SELF-STORAGE THE JOURNEY

THE HOTTEST SMALL BUSINESS OPPORTUNITY IN AMERICA

Dean Brown

INTRODUCTION

Are you interested in the Self-Storage Industry?

This book is your introduction to the Self-Storage Industry. It covers its origin, current state, and future prospects.

Whether it's your dream or you're already involved, this book offers valuable insights and guidance.

Backed by research from industry experts and professionals across America, it addresses common questions like how to get started, where to find information, and potential investment. For those already in the business, it also provides strategies for growth, sale, or financial planning."

It is still one of the most exceptional business opportunities in America today. If you are thinking about getting involved, you probably have a lot of questions.

We have researched and prepared this book utilizing information received from owners and operators as well as from builders, contractors, and developers across America.

TABLE OF CONTENTS

CHAPTER 1

THE BIRTH OF SELF-STORAGE

After the end of World War II, Self-Storage emerged as a solution for military personnel who needed space to store their belongings.

As the demand for storage increased, people turned to their friends who had extra garage space to accommodate their excess items.

This was also the time when America became more mobile with the construction of new highways and an increase in income, leading to a culture of consumerism.

As a result, people started accumulating more possessions than they needed. However, over time, this generation realized the need for a better solution as their homes lacked basements and attics to store their excess belongings.

This gave rise to the self-storage concept, a true testament to American ingenuity, which has evolved into the successful business it is today.

A handful of enterprising individuals embarked on constructing basic concrete block buildings with roll-up doors - the issue being the frequent occurrence of cracks and leaks in such structures.

As time passed, the need for constant sealing and painting of these buildings prompted a quest for a more efficient option.

It was during this search that someone stumbled upon metal buildings, which seemed to be the ideal solution. The 1970s saw a surge in the construction of metal buildings, but they were nowhere near as advanced as they are now.

This period also marked the rise of numerous metal building companies, as they were a more affordable and low-maintenance alternative. However, the earlier versions of these buildings were made with thicker galvanized steel, making them susceptible to rust. The tell-tale sight of the powdery white substance that appears on aging buildings is all too familiar.

For nearly four decades, American businesses have been targeting the Baby Boomer generation, who have been spending exorbitant amounts of money on homes, luxuries, and everyday necessities.

With such lavish expenditures, the challenge of secure storage facilities emerged. One would assume that their purchases would eventually reach a limit, but the opposite occurred. The competition to possess the latest and greatest items was fueled by clever marketing tactics, enticing individuals to acquire items they couldn't live without.

At the turn of the century, the Baby Boomers began to reach the age of retirement. However, a significant portion of this generation is not simply spending their leisure time traveling in RVs or playing golf. In fact, a large number of them are venturing into entrepreneurship.

An investigation by the Ewing Marion Kaufman Foundation revealed that individuals between 55 and 64 years old are the most likely to start a new business in America. This phenomenon is gaining momentum.

After dedicating many years to working for others, they now yearn to work for themselves. Unlike younger individuals, they possess the resources and expertise to pursue this path.

For many aspiring entrepreneurs, the self-storage industry is an attractive option for a post-retirement career. It is one of the few small business opportunities that offer low-risk and high-reward prospects.

One of the reasons for this is the vast network of contacts these Baby Boomers have cultivated throughout their corporate careers. They believe that this network can be leveraged to fuel their ideas and businesses in their retirement years. For those with an entrepreneurial drive, the self-storage industry provides a perfect outlet.

This industry has experienced tremendous growth, with self-storage businesses in the United States.

Interestingly, the offspring of Baby Boomers, born between the late 1970s and early 1990s, have adopted similar spending habits as their parents. They now contribute to an annual spending of over $170 billion, and with a population of over 70 million, they are beginning to catch up with the 80 million Baby Boomers.

This new market is shaping consumer behavior, attitudes, and society in general. A substantial number of these individuals reside in apartments, limiting their storage space significantly. This trend has contributed to the growth of self-storage businesses, with two groups, namely the military and students, being the primary users.

While the use of self-storage among students is on the rise, the Iraq war has caused an increase in the utilization of self-storage facilities by military personnel. Approximately 3% of the industry is attributed to the military, who often require storage for their belongings while relocating or serving overseas for extended periods.

Frequently, these individuals have no control over their schedule and are given short notice for their orders, which adds to the burden of organizing their affairs. To assist these customers, most operators go out of their way to provide extra support by extending late payment notifications.

Thus, it is essential to market self-storage to both groups - students can benefit during their college years, while military personnel can enjoy the convenience of storage.

The self-storage industry has evolved significantly, with drive-up, drive-through, climate-controlled, multi-story units, and even specialized features such as wine cellars, gun safes, and vaults. If you look around, you will likely find a demand for storage in your community. In fact, storage facilities are now being built to blend seamlessly into neighborhoods, some even incorporating luxurious living spaces.

This book will reveal how these buildings have become both aesthetically pleasing and practical, leaving you with one burning question: How could any business-minded entrepreneur pass up such a lucrative opportunity? It is highly recommended to join the ranks of the over 40,000 facilities in this industry and consider it a wise investment. Despite the numerous acquisitions by larger companies, the "mom and pop facilities" still dominate the market.

In fact, Prudential Real Estate Investors has identified the self-storage industry as a highly desirable investment option. Over the past decade, this industry has undergone significant changes, with five companies going public, one transitioning from public to private ownership, and another being acquired by a market leader.

While these transactions have totaled over four billion dollars, they only represent a fraction of the industry's total market share. To put this into perspective, the top fifteen operators in the country own less than seventeen percent of the mainstream market. This lack of consolidation is one of the main reasons why the self-storage industry is one of the most sought-after investment opportunities in America, offering a high-quality product with the potential to generate significant profits.

Three Unique Categories of Self-Storage Investors and Builders:

1. REITs (Real Estate Investment Trusts) have experienced growth in recent years, prompting larger investors (many of whom are not traditionally involved in self-storage) to shift their focus towards this industry. Some are even forming partnerships with smaller operations in order to pursue larger deals and expand their portfolio.

2. Emerging individuals with no prior involvement in self-storage are now drawn to the industry as they become aware of its lucrative returns. With a background in other areas of real estate such as industrial or retail sectors, they are now venturing into self-storage as well.

3. Some are acquiring existing self-storage facilities to enter a new market, while others

are choosing to develop their own facility from the ground up.

Some Important Factors to Consider: If you are contemplating a career as a developer in this industry, it is crucial to be diligent and conduct thorough research on new projects. It is essential to have a thorough understanding of the field. Instead of just focusing on the specifics of a project, it is important to analyze the industry as a whole and make an informed decision.

Every aspect of a new project must be carefully considered. It is crucial to examine the potential customer base, the specific market area, and the existing and future competition.

Next, consider the location. Explore the diverse opportunities available and educate yourself on any potential areas of interest. The site **selection process is of utmost importance** and requires careful attention.

Conduct feasibility and market studies with great care. In today's constantly evolving market, interest and capitalization rates play a significant role. It is important for the financial institutions that developers rely on for loans to have a thorough understanding of the industry, including cash flow, lease-up, and the overall process of constructing a facility from start to finish.

A developer must also consider facility management and operations early on in the development process. Hiring experienced industry managers can greatly contribute to the success of a project.

If your plan involves constructing a larger facility, it is crucial for the manager to have knowledge of self-storage.

Their responsibilities would include leasing space, marketing, retail sales, and ancillary services. It is advisable to involve this person in the process early on to assess their suitability for the role. They may also have valuable insights to aid in the process and can assist with setting up and managing the choice, reservation, or leasing of space, as well as supporting the grand opening.

Overall, the "build it, and they will come" approach is not a viable one. Adopting this mindset can lead to project failure. The more you educate yourself during this process, the better equipped you will be for profitability.

In the US, there are over 40,000 facilities, and in this industry, strategic planning is just as important for newcomers as it is for experienced operators and self-storage REITs.

However, simply investing in self-storage does not guarantee success. One must carefully consider site feasibility and location, as we will discuss in Chapter 5.

Despite the comparable rents to apartment ownership, self-storage offers fewer hassles with operations and management, making it a solid investment. Over time, the self-storage industry has evolved and is now highly sought after by sophisticated investors who recognize its potential.

While for many years few facilities were available for sale due to satisfied owners, the recent expansion boom has opened up new opportunities.

Are you interested in a self-storage facility? What was once considered a secondary real estate investment category, self-storage is now at the forefront of the commercial real estate market.

Some buyers are choosing to consolidate their operations, while others are purchasing these properties. The industry is currently experiencing its most active investment market ever, with Self-Storage REITs only accounting for about 5% of the equity REIT market but boasting one of the highest 10-year compound annual return rates.

This increased interest is fueled by favorable cap rates, which are higher than other asset classes and make self-storage a "core asset" according to Wall Street.

It's A Lucrative Investment Opportunity:

What other factors contribute to the profitability of the self-storage industry?

Compared to many other businesses, the failure rate is significantly lower.

Additionally, your facility will generate returns in a relatively short period, especially when compared to more traditional enterprises.

Are you in your golden years? If so, this could be an ideal venture for you to consider. According to the 2006 Merrill Lynch New Retirement Study, one of the fastest growing groups of entrepreneurs in the U.S. are Baby Boomers in search of their ideal retirement. They are looking for a "retirement career" that will keep them mentally and physically engaged.

The self-storage industry is on the rise and presents a promising opportunity for this growing demographic.

Starting a new business always involves risks that must be carefully evaluated before diving into entrepreneurship. However, self-storage steel buildings have shown to have a more promising track record compared to other commercial ventures.

According to a comprehensive study by National Development Services Inc. on the performance of various developments in multiple states, self-storage steel buildings have only an 8% failure rate. In contrast, other real estate ventures have a much higher failure rate, ranging from 53% to 63%.

A Positive Outlook for the Future: What can we expect in the near future? The outlook is positive. As economic concerns continue to grow, investing in a secure and long-term venture becomes even more appealing.

The latest "Confidence Index" from the Mini-Storage Messenger shows a slight increase in rental trends and excellent confidence in the self-storage industry.

This optimism further reinforces the notion that self-storage is less susceptible to economic pressures compared to other businesses and real estate sectors. The report also highlights a slight increase in occupancy rates and unchanged capital expenditures, while declining interest rates make the investment even more attractive.

Investing in self-storage steel buildings also involves a smaller initial cost compared to other new businesses. With a 75-80% occupancy rate and factoring in land purchase, materials, and construction, one can expect to pay off their loan within six years.

This is a significantly shorter time frame compared to most other small businesses. Moreover, if you already own the land and build self-storage buildings on it, you are ahead of the game. With the same occupancy rate, it would only take two and a half to three years to break even and start seeing substantial profits.

Additionally, this business does not require a large staff to maintain. It is highly likely that you will be able to manage the facility with just a few employees for day-to-day operations.

After years of working in large buildings with thousands of other people, who wouldn't want the freedom and limited responsibility that comes with managing a self-storage facility? Join a Thriving Industry: Investing in self-storage means becoming part of a growing industry with a proven demand.

It has been the fastest-growing sector of the commercial real estate industry for the past 30 years.

Self-storage is not only a stable industry but a **steadily growing one with demonstrated demand**. In addition to consumers, businesses also require storage. They need storage for surplus choice supplies as well as equipment while moving.

A leveraged self-storage property typically breaks even at an occupancy rate of 60-72%, while leveraged multi-family, choice, and retail properties require a higher break-even occupancy rate of 80-90%.

This indicates that self-storage properties have a greater capacity to withstand market downturns.

Furthermore, the total development cost of self-storage properties is significantly lower compared to multi-family, choice, or retail properties, resulting in a lower investment or loan amount for investors.

This advantage is reflected in the comparable rents among different real estate investments. Moreover, the operating and management costs of self-storage facilities are considerably lower.

Unlike apartments or retail properties, self-storage facilities do not require constant maintenance of grounds, appliances, plumbing, and other amenities that often require full-time staff.

In terms of tenant turnover, self-storage properties are more convenient and less labor-intensive to manage, with only one or two managers overseeing the facility. This results in fewer "headaches" associated with managing tenants, as compared to "live-in" units.

From an investor's perspective, the potential for higher ROI (return on investment) is a significant advantage of self-storage properties over other real estate investments.

Additionally, the initial investment required for self-storage properties is only a fraction of what is needed for other properties. Due to the lower break-even occupancy rates, investors can anticipate lower risks during economic downturns, which can affect occupancy rates and rental prices.

Furthermore, investors do not have to worry about additional capital requirements for tenant improvements or ongoing maintenance costs.

Overall, operating a self-storage facility is less labor-intensive and requires fewer expenses for heating, electrical, plumbing, and HVAC maintenance.

According to the Mini-Storage Messenger, capital expenditures for tenant turnover are also significantly lower, as there are no real estate commissions to be paid. In most cases, preparing a unit for a new tenant only requires basic cleaning.

Don't Underestimate the Potential of Small Towns: The possibilities in small towns can be quite grand. In fact, many locally owned self-storage facilities have thrived in non-metropolitan areas.

And as these smaller communities continue to flourish, these facilities will also thrive alongside them. After all, the cost of land in these areas is much more reasonable compared to larger cities.

I have also observed that farmers and landowners on the outskirts of town have ventured into this industry because the major start-up cost, which is the land, was already taken care of. Instead of relying solely on crops, they realized they could have a year-round source of income with less effort.

It became apparent that owning their own land was a huge advantage in this venture. And as their town grew, so did their exposure. With the majority of Americans residing in metropolitan areas, many are becoming fed up with the drawbacks that come with that environment.

As a result, more and more people are moving to rural and suburban areas, with a significant number choosing smaller towns.

It's no secret that they desire a lower crime rate, less noise, affordable prices, and less traffic. Even big businesses are following this trend. They are finding that regulations are less stringent and the cost of conducting business in these smaller cities is lower.

A prime example is Wal-Mart, which has long recognized the potential of establishing stores in smaller towns. Another important trend is the shift from manufacturing and farming to a more service-based economy in smaller communities. This brings about innovative thinking, as seen in some entrepreneurs building self-storage facilities in multiple small towns within a state or 150-mile radius of a major city.

These facilities typically only have a phone connection that rings to a central location (often the owner's home). Once they gather the customer's information and credit card details, they provide a gate code and mail a contract, which the customer must sign and return.

In these markets, competition is scarce, making it easier to identify potential competing facilities. It's important to consult with local developers to determine the best neighborhoods and growth areas.

And don't forget to do thorough research.

Even during market fluctuations, the self-storage industry continues to thrive. The concept of supply and demand is highly relevant, as the demand for self-storage remains consistently high.

While there may be some peaks and valleys, the demand still surpasses the supply, particularly for RV storage.

In the current market, while short-term funds have decreased, long-term funds have seen an increase, making it more beneficial for storage owners to refinance or acquire property.

When faced with this decision, they must choose between locking in a fixed rate for a period of 5 to 10 years or opting for a shorter-term loan with a variable rate. The latter option allows for the flexibility to prepay, and also provides the opportunity to take advantage of potential market downturns in interest rates. This presents a prime opportunity for storage owners to boost their income through expansion or by implementing rent increases. This in turn sets the stage for potential future refinancing or sale of the business.

CHAPTER 2

BUILD OR PURCHASE

There are several reasons why some self-storage owners choose to sell their facilities. Some are concerned about the expansion of the market, while others simply want to liquidate their properties while the market is at its peak.

Buyers are eager to invest in self-storage facilities due to the positive reputation of this industry. The ease of management, flexibility in rent increases, and lower construction costs are some of the main factors that attract buyers to these facilities.

It is important to note that self-storage facilities differ from residential properties, and therefore require a thorough analysis of the specific details related to this industry.

Setting up a self-storage business is more complex than most other industries, so it is crucial to do thorough research and gain familiarity with the industry.

Modern self-storage facilities often generate additional income, making it even more important for potential buyers to have a broad understanding of the industry.

Before entering into a purchasing contract, it is essential to verify all the information gathered during the investigation.

This includes visiting the local police departments to inquire about any incidents or calls made to the facility in the past few years. A history of thefts and break-ins could suggest potential challenges in marketing the facility.

It is also important to inspect the physical condition of the building(s) and review the lease agreements. The lease agreements should contain all necessary information to hold tenants accountable, and it is also important to ensure that they comply with state statutes to avoid any legal issues.

Some sellers may intentionally avoid auctions to maintain high occupancy rates, making it crucial to thoroughly review files and documentation procedures.

As the new owner, you do not want to inherit any legal issues resulting from previous mismanagement.

During your examination of the financial records, be sure to review the profit and loss statements for the past three years. Give equal attention to the balance sheets, payment histories, and tax returns.

It is important to also inquire about the current owners' insurance policies and thoroughly review the loan documents, title policy, deeds of trust, and notes.

If necessary, seek guidance from a realtor or attorney to ensure everything is in proper order. Verify the validity of each customer and their rental agreements to avoid inheriting any incorrect information and potentially selling their property.

Consider researching the facility's competitors and investigating the reputation of the business that has caught your interest. What are others saying about the facility and its current owner?

Constructing a Self-Storage Facility:

The cost of constructing a self-storage facility is significantly lower compared to building prime or commercial spaces, hotels, or multi-family residences. In most instances, the construction expenses, including land and soft costs (fees, financing, and payments to various advisors or experts), amount to only one-third of the cost of other real estate types.

Unlike constructing apartments, there is minimal installation of plumbing and electrical systems in a self-storage facility. The interior space is relatively uniform, with predetermined unit sizes rather than complex residential floor plans. This means less drywalling and finishing work is needed. One must consider customization options since individual tenants often require specific unit features to suit their needs.

However, in general, these elements make developing self-storage facilities a less daunting task. Once a self-storage facility is established, it is significantly less labor-intensive to operate and maintain.

The staff is usually limited to you and a few employees, a manager, or a couple. A part-time assistant manager may also be considered.

There are no real estate commissions to pay, and when a tenant vacates, it usually involves simple tasks like sweeping out the unit.

The good news is that self-storage facilities generate the same rent per square foot as apartments. Specialty storage options can even fetch higher rates. Moreover, self-storage facilities have lower delinquency rates, and rents can be increased more easily.

When the rent is raised by five percent, tenants would rather pay the extra amount than go through the hassle of moving.

Looking towards the future, self-storage will remain a popular choice for residential customers. Additionally, the demand for self-storage among commercial tenants is growing. It is more cost-effective for them to rent a storage space at a facility rather than a more expensive prime space. This trend is only expected to become more appealing.

People are constantly acquiring more belongings, both personal and commercial, expanding their operations with more equipment or inventory, starting home-based businesses, or simply needing extra storage space. These individuals will continue to turn to self-storage to fulfill their requirements.

With this information in mind, you can now decide on the type of facility you want to build or purchase.

Some options to consider include:

- Basic Dry Storage Only

- Climate Control

- Basic RV and Boat Storage

- Condominium Style RV and Boat Storage

- Conversion

- Mobile Self-Storage

- Multi-Story Self-Storage

- Private Storage in Multi-Family Buildings

- Records Storage

- Wine Storage

- Combination of Retail and Self-Storage Plan

Your Exit Strategy: If you are considering buying or building a self-storage facility, it is essential to plan your exit strategy. This strategy may change over time, but it is necessary to be well-prepared for any future developments.

Would it be more beneficial for me to Refinance or Sell?

In this competitive lending market, refinancing could be a wise decision to take advantage of attractive interest rates.

On the other hand, the current demand for self-storage real estate is surpassing the supply, making it a prime time to sell your property in the competitive market.

Contrary to popular belief, you don't need to have a near-perfect occupancy rate to consider selling your facility. However, it is recommended to have at least 60% occupancy before listing it for sale.

The past few years have shown great success for those who have sold their investments, as the self-storage market is currently one of the most lucrative industries. More investors are now interested in self-storage properties due to the clear advantages.

However, it is crucial to thoroughly research and seek guidance from a real estate advisor who is knowledgeable about both selling and refinancing markets and has no vested interest in your decision.

Always have a plan in place to run your facility efficiently and aim for growth, as this will increase its value and attract potential buyers, whether it is a family member, employee, or third-party.

When building a self-storage facility, it is likely to attract institutional investors, so it is essential to have added value and a prime location with functional units to make it an attractive purchase.

Another option for exit strategy is the tax-deferred 1031 Exchange. As per the Internal Revenue Code Section 1031, if you exchange your property for a "like-kind" property, you can delay paying taxes.

When considering whether to sell your property for cash, pay taxes and depart completely, or accept stock options and hope for appreciation on Wall Street, keep in mind that the main advantage of selling to a public company is the deferral of taxes.

Additionally, it is crucial to present effective financial controls to convince potential buyers that your company's financial statements accurately represent its financial standing.

To maximize the value of your self-storage property and attract eager investors, thorough research and understanding of the market is essential before deciding to sell.

Remember that each self-storage market is unique, and it is important to assess the local economy and make decisions based on long-term growth opportunities.

It is crucial to have a grasp on the local landscape and trends in your city or market.

This will help you determine if selling your property is a viable option in terms of cash flow, your financial situation, and the structure of the local market.

If you decide that selling your property is the best course of action, it is important to make necessary repairs and thoroughly clean the facility. This will help attract potential buyers.

For instance, if your goal is to build and sell the property, it is wise to target a broader market rather than a more limited one.

In today's market, technology plays a significant role in the success of self-storage facilities.

Therefore, it is crucial to understand which technological aspects are crucial for modern self-storage facilities and whether your potential buyer has a desire for advanced technology.

When preparing to sell your property, it is important to have detailed reports readily available. Potential investors will want to see at least three years' worth of accounting records, including income statements, occupancy and rent rates, and expenses.

It is also necessary to provide a reasonable revenue projection for the next three years. In conclusion, selling your self-storage property requires careful consideration and preparation.

By understanding the market, making necessary improvements, and providing detailed reports, you can attract the right buyers and maximize the value of your property.

The Significance of Establishing Value:

The concept behind your plan is to establish substantial value in your property during your ownership. This will allow you to present an appealing investment to the market, one that yields significant returns upon its sale.

Once you have diligently completed all necessary preparations and are ready to meet your investors' expectations with success, you will be well on your way to securing the highest selling price for your self-storage facility.

However, as mentioned earlier, it is crucial to consider an exit strategy from the outset, so you do not miss out on any opportunities that may arise.

CHAPTER 3

TYPES OF FACILITIES

1. **Basic Dry Storage:**

This type of storage facility offers dry units in various sizes, including 5x5, 5x10, 10x10, and 10x20.

2. **Climate-Control:**

The Value of Climate Control. What it means to your business and your bottom line. A little more cost to build, but the rewards far outweigh those costs.

Despite its name, Climate Control storage does not always live up to its title. It would be more accurate to call it Temperature Control.

Let's explore the value of climate regulation, which has become a growing trend in the search for storage facilities that can safeguard personal belongings from extreme temperatures.

Customers are willing to go the extra mile to find a facility that offers such units. They are seeking a solution for storing items that require specific temperature and humidity levels.

This consumer demand gained prominence in the late 1990s, prompting facilities to include at least a couple of climate-controlled units in their inventory.

However, as these units quickly filled up, the focus shifted towards constructing entire buildings dedicated to climate control.

Maintaining a temperature below 90 degrees in the summer and above 40 degrees in the winter, along with humidity levels below 65%, which is crucial in these units. A reliable dehumidification system is essential in achieving this. To ensure optimal humidity control, air-conditioning loads should be designed at a rate of 1500 square feet per ton, which is considerably lower than that of a typical home or apartment.

It may be necessary to initially offer discounted rates to attract customers, but as they recognize the value of these units, lease rates can be increased. As demand continues to rise, adjusting prices can lead to improved profitability.

Effective management is crucial in regulating the heat, cooling, and humidity levels. To ensure continuous protection for your units, having a backup generator is an excellent solution. It is important to regularly monitor or have alarms in place to alert you if the set limits are exceeded for temperature and humidity. This aspect should be clearly articulated in your rental agreement or lease.

Your lease should also have provisions to address situations where the systems for temperature and climate control may fail due to circumstances beyond your control, such as blackouts, tornadoes, or other disasters.

In this summary, it is stated that any owner or representative of a personal property storage facility cannot claim it to be "climate controlled" without specifying the temperature and humidity range maintained. Failure to do so or to maintain the advertised range will result in a misdemeanor charge and liability for any damage caused to the occupant's property.

It is important to advertise services with honesty, specifying if only heating or cooling is available, or both with a controlled dehumidification system.

There is no need for your air conditioner to run in the early morning when the temperature is cooler. While it extracts moisture during the day, it accumulates it at night. dehumidifiers air conditioner and dehumidifier work together to maintain a comfortable environment.

By reducing humidity levels to five percent, the air conditioner can function more efficiently without wasting fifty percent of its energy on removing water. It is most effective when cooling dry air, while the dehumidifier works better when drying cool air.

A professional can assist in determining the most efficient HVAC and dehumidification system for your building(s).

In terms of marketing, highlight the design, reliability, and other advantages of climate control units.

Some customers, particularly pharmaceutical representatives, may require certification of maintenance procedures. Keep records and install alarms to alert when limits are exceeded.

3 **RV and Boat Storage**:

Facilities for Storing RVs and Boats:

You must determine the most suitable storage space for your project. There are five options available for storing RVs and boats, and you may consider including one of these facilities in your overall site.

Typically, RV storage is planned at a ratio of 30 to 50 units per acre, with a 60-degree parking angle being the most suitable.

This design allows for narrower driveways, reducing the need for a 60-foot driveway to only 30 to 50 feet. However, the only concern is ensuring that the doors function properly at this angle.

Another innovative way to save space is by using RV covers, similar to carports. These are popular amenities as they can be rented at a higher rate compared to open designs, and they do not require concrete.

In some areas of the country, gravel or asphalt are popular choices. Additionally, building with these materials costs about half the price of enclosed units.

Moreover, by using steel fencing along the property line, the RV can be hidden from the street and give the appearance of a fully enclosed building.

It is crucial to analyze the economics and determine if the proposed project is financially feasible. Will the rental prices be sufficient to cover the expenses of the land and construction?

Consider the market and assess whether it is oversaturated or if there is room for another RV and boat storage facility. It is also essential to address any potential zoning challenges and evaluate the topography of the site to see if it is suitable for storage.

When it comes to boats, the expenses associated with wet storage (boats in slips on the lake) may not be justified by the convenience factor.

Dry storage is a more cost-effective option, especially in a well-chosen location. An excellent utilization of space is by stacking smaller boats.

The new lift system, developed by Harold Leslie of Leslie Industries in Florida, allows for storage of six to seven boats in the same amount of space as one boat.

4. Conversions:

Conversions involve repurposing existing buildings into storage facilities. Warehouses, factories, and retail structures, among others, can be converted into storage units. The trend of converting larger buildings, such as those over 100,000 square feet, has increased in recent years.

These buildings often come fully equipped with amenities such as heating, air-conditioning, elevators, and high security features. Additionally, they offer prime advertising space and can be renovated and occupied quickly.

When considering a conversion or building a new facility, location is crucial. Look for areas with favorable traffic patterns and easy access. Zoning is typically not an issue, as more developers are choosing conversions over ground-up developments.

In many cases, municipalities are supportive of converting abandoned buildings into functional storage facilities due to the increased tax revenue and improved appearance.

One benefit of converting an existing building into a self-storage facility is the time saved on dealing with building departments and zoning boards, as the building is already zoned and ready for use. This can result in a project being completed in 70% less time than usual.

Another crucial factor to consider is the functionality and strength of the elevators, as they must be able to transport both individuals and their belongings. The elevator doors should also be appropriately sized, and the elevators should be within 150 feet of the farthest storage unit.

A more economical alternative is a Vertical Reciprocating Conveyor (VRC), also known as a storage lift, material lift, freight lift, or cargo lift. These can be easily installed in any building and have a reliable safety record, at half the cost of elevators.

However, if the building has four or more levels or must comply with the American with Disabilities Act, a passenger elevator may be necessary for customer convenience.

The HVAC system should also be evaluated, especially if climate-controlled storage is offered. It is recommended to consult with an experienced architect before proceeding with the conversion process, as it can be a profitable venture.

Constructing Multi-Level Storage Buildings: Despite the challenges they may present, multi-story buildings are now a more viable option due to rising land costs and limited availability. While this approach can help offset the expense of purchasing land, it is crucial to carefully consider all additional costs before making the investment.

This is where a feasibility study proves to be extremely valuable. In many cases, opting for a larger plot of land instead of a smaller one can generate significant savings that can then be allocated towards a multi-story structure.

Once the decision to build upwards is made, the question arises - how many levels should be constructed?

The primary consideration is whether to go with two stories or opt for three or more. The goal should be to maximize the rental space's value on a particular site. The foundation of a multi-story building must include full footings, unlike single-story structures.

Furthermore, incorporating second or third-floor slabs increases the cost of concrete. Another important decision to make is whether to install one or two elevators, a material lift, or a combination of both.

Codes and regulations, including fire exits and emergency alarms, must also be considered, making the expertise of an engineer and architect invaluable.

These professionals are well-versed in all local and state guidelines and are familiar with the Americans with Disabilities Act (ADA) statutes. It is essential to keep in mind that these expenses can be significant, depending on the state's requirements. Additionally, providing elevators can substantially raise electrical costs.

5 **Mobile Storage**:

This type of service involves the transportation of individual storage containers to and from homes and businesses for storage at your facility or for moving purposes.

The self-storage industry is currently deliberating on the viability of incorporating mobile storage into their business. However, with its increasing popularity, many see it as a strategic way to enhance their operations and stand out from competitors.

Since its emergence in 2001, this approach has been gaining traction and is expected to compete with the traditional moving industry and rental trucks. However, it does require more space and resources, which can increase overhead costs.

To venture into this area, thorough research is necessary, along with excellent management skills.

While self-storage is often seen as a real estate venture, mobile storage is more of a service-oriented business. It may take longer to rent a portable storage unit compared to a traditional on-site unit, and proper consumer education and marketing are crucial.

However, it does expand the range of your operations. This service is best suited for larger self-storage facilities, but it is possible to start small and gradually expand. If interested, it's essential to act quickly as competitors may take advantage of this opportunity.

As the demand for mobile storage increases, a full-time delivery and pick-up person will be necessary, and managing this aspect will require a detail-oriented and organized manager.

Fortunately, there are software programs available to streamline the operations of a mobile storage business.

Most operators have a minimum rental period for these units, and it's essential to consider the fuel costs when setting delivery rates. Customers often use these units for moving, which requires a team of two people.

The most critical aspect of mobile storage is the lift system, which must be efficient, reliable, and able to withstand any weather conditions.

Customers expect timely and professional service, so it's crucial to research and invest in the best lift system for your business.

One crucial element to consider is the container or box for your business. You may be wondering which type is optimal. It is essential to devise a plan for selecting the appropriate size and type.

How many options should you have? As you fill about 20 containers, it is wise to order more. Kontane, a company with no minimum purchase requirement, offers discounts for larger orders.

However, keep in mind that to see a profitable outcome, you will eventually need over 100 containers.

There are metal containers, which are pricier than wood or plastic, but they are also more durable. Some can even be taken apart and stacked when not in use.

However, storing these containers requires careful planning. If you plan on stacking them, you will need a forklift capable of lifting over 10,000 pounds at least 15 feet high. While the industry standard size is 8 feet by 5 feet by 7 feet, there are various sizes available.

It is crucial to choose a practical and economically sound option for your space. Research thoroughly, and you will find numerous companies online offering mobile choices, trailers, and overseas shipping containers.

As this idea is relatively new, it is crucial to remain aware of any changing legal issues. You will be responsible for storing your customers' personal belongings, so it is essential to uphold that responsibility.

While the self-storage business primarily deals with real estate transactions, mobile storage is involved in both the rental and transportation of personal property.

In the future, the portable storage industry will have a clear definition of its operations and role. It is crucial to familiarize yourself with the transportation and storage laws in your area.

Some states have minimal regulations, while others have strict guidelines. Depending on your state, you may need a license as a warehouseman to transport customers' goods, and specific regulations must be followed. It is vital to do your research in this area, as knowledge is key.

Furthermore, it is important to have the right insurance coverage. If the self-storage facility is not at fault, the customer is responsible for insurance for their belongings while stored on your premises.

To protect yourself, consider including a clause in your rental agreement stating that customers cannot store more than $5,000 worth of goods in their container. This approach will safeguard your business in case of any unfortunate incidents.

6. **Outdoor Storage**:

The open storage space ranges from 10 feet by 20 feet to 12 feet by 50 feet. This strictly offers outdoor parking with individual spaces allocated either on the blacktop or through a marking system.

However, this provides no protection from the elements, and the storage area must be maintained orderly to minimize accidents.

The spaces should be numbered and assigned, with extra room for overflow parking. This option is also ideal for phased development.

7. **Covered Space**:

These are open spaces with a roof, known as carports, and are more profitable than the open storage option. You can offer both open and covered spaces, giving customers a choice based on their preferences.

Although building a covered space is more expensive, the protection it offers allows for higher rental charges.

8. **Canopy with Walls**:

This option includes canopy storage with end walls, providing two-sided storage.

In areas with high wind and snow levels, three-sided storage is recommended. It can be constructed in long rows within the facility or along the perimeter wall, providing partially covered parking by enclosing the back and both ends.

This works best when the RVs can be backed into space, providing protection from the sun.

9. **Indoor Storage:**

This involves fully enclosed spaces, but it is the least efficient use of land. It is suitable for storing expensive RVs and can offer additional amenities such as climate control, automatic doors, and electricity.

Private storage within multi-family buildings is a valuable option for families who require additional storage space but lack room in their living quarters. These storage units can be conveniently located in a central area, such as the basement, for easy access by residents.

In high-density cities like New York City, this trend is becoming more popular due to the convenience and cost-savings compared to external storage options.

Even building developers are incorporating these storage areas into their plans, with various options such as wire-mesh or fully enclosed units. It is clear that the demand for in-house storage facilities is on the rise, and it is a smart move for building developers to consider including them in their designs.

5. **Condo-Style Storage**:

This is the future of RV storage, where units are sold, and different levels of service are charged. These units usually have 14-foot-wide bays and come with several amenities, including a luxurious clubhouse, specialty café, RV washes, valet, and make-ready services, which can boost your profits.

No matter what type of RV and boat storage you prefer (such as Condominium Style RV and Boat Storage), there are certain key factors to consider.

As stated in a press release by the RVIA (Recreational Vehicle Industry Association), there has been a significant increase in RV shipments in the past few years.

This indicates a strong market, with projections showing continued growth.

Land Costs and Size Considerations: Constructing a multi-level condominium-style facility for RV and boat storage is no easy feat. It requires finding suitable land at a reasonable price, with a minimum of seven acres.

Maximizing the efficiency of the purchased land is essential for the profitability of the project. This means that if the land is costly, careful market analysis is necessary.

Fortunately, the latest zoning ordinances have begun to recognize the value and benefits of RV and boat storage, especially in addressing the issue of parking in residential areas. These facilities contribute to the overall well-being of the community.

What is the Shape of the Land? The layout's efficiency is determined by the land's shape. Generally, a rectangular lot is more effective than a square one.

The site is most efficient when the driver can easily drive through with access on both sides. The main focus should be on accommodating RVs and vehicles towing boats.

Another important factor is circulation, which influences the size of the site. Consider how much space is needed for a truck and a boat to circulate and how long the rig is. It is crucial to thoroughly research construction and soft costs and ensure that the contractor you choose has the necessary level of expertise.

Ensuring strong security measures is imperative: Prevention is more effective than apprehension. There is a diverse range of security devices available, such as fences, lighting, computerized gate entry, surveillance cameras, and individual alarms for boats and RVs.

Incorporating motion sensors and offering them as an additional feature for customers at an extra cost of $10 per month is recommended. It is also wise to install door alarms for enclosed units.

Strategically placing digital video cameras that activate upon detecting movement at all entrances and exits is crucial. The quality of the equipment must be exceptional to capture license plates and clear facial features.

Instead of concealing the cameras, it is advisable to make them conspicuous as it can act as a deterrent. Photoelectric beams along the fences can detect any intrusions.

However, it is essential to be cautious while using the term "surveillance" in marketing and discussions with customers.

Some states prohibit the use of this language unless there is continuous patrolling on the premises.

One significant advantage of using photoelectric beams is that they can prevent potential criminals from becoming tenants to gain access to the property.

It is crucial to implement a policy in the lease/rental contract that requires a tenant exiting after closing hours to contact the police. This can help establish a positive relationship with the local police department.

When a would-be thief posing as a tenant is aware of this policy, they are less likely to stay after hours. Conducting rounds on all parts of the property just after closing is recommended. Using "key access" dumpsters and placing them near the entrance can help deter thieves.

If possible, eliminating dumpsters altogether can prevent thieves from using them to store stolen property for later retrieval. Adequate lighting is essential as thieves often prefer to operate in the dark. Individual door alarms are also effective in deterring criminal activity.

Having proper fire protection measures in place is a must, including up-to-date fire extinguishers and water access.

Insurance coverage for RV and boat storage can be complex and requires careful consideration. It is crucial to have adequate and appropriate insurance in place for your storage facility.

One option to consider is a comprehensive business owner's policy, which offers protection against property loss and damage.

Additionally, liability coverage for bodily injury and property damage, as well as loss of income due to such incidents, is crucial. You should also have specialized coverage for customers' goods and sale and disposal legal liability.

When offering condominium-style RV and boat storage, it is essential to consult with your insurance agent to ensure you have the necessary coverage.

Your standard self-storage rental agreement may need to be modified to accommodate this type of specialized storage.

Improving Rental Agreements for RV, Boat, and Vehicle Storage: Customize your rental terms and conditions to cater specifically to the storage of RVs, boats, and vehicles.

Accurate information about the stored vehicle, including its year, make, model, license plate, and VIN, is crucial for handling abandoned items. It is important to obtain a copy of the registration and a detailed description of the stored item.

Make sure that the name on the registration matches the person signing the rental agreement.

Additionally, require the tenant to provide proof of insurance with appropriate property and liability coverage. In case of a fire, it is vital to prevent it from spreading to other vehicles.

To ensure a smooth storage process, the rental agreements should include the following points:

- A clear and specific identification of the stored item.

- A clause stating that only the identified item can be parked in the designated space.

- Maintenance of records for the registration and title of the stored item.

- Proof of insurance from the tenant for their vehicle.

- Adherence to gas tank rules and regulations.

- Strictly prohibiting any oil changes or repairs on the property.

- Establishing a protocol for handling hazardous materials such as gas and oil.

- Emphasizing the importance of parking in designated spaces for all customers.

- Addressing any potential loopholes in the rental agreement that may be exploited by tenants' attorneys.

- Providing overflow parking options and implementing consequences for tenants who park incorrectly.

It is crucial to review and revise the rental agreements with the help of a legal professional to avoid any legal complications. By implementing these measures, you can ensure a hassle-free storage experience for both you and your tenants.

Solving Parking Problems:

According to Chip Cordes, representative of U.S. Door & Building Components, the main issue arises when units are positioned at an angle, requiring wider piers between the doors to accommodate the necessary backroom for roll-up doors.

Typically, 24-inch-wide piers are sufficient, but the angle of the units must be considered, with most not exceeding a 30 percent angle from the driveway.

Another approach is to create a saw-tooth pattern in the building, although this can be more expensive to construct. When it comes to storage for RVs and boats, the type of door used is a crucial factor.

Sectional doors are not suitable for angled storage, leaving chain-hoisted or motorized doors as the remaining options. With chain-hoisted doors, tenants must physically open the roll-up door and enter inside to reach the chain hoist, leading many facility operators to install a pedestrian door next to the roll-up door.

To address this issue, U.S. Door & Building Components has developed the EZ-Access Roll-up Door, which features a walk-through pedestrian door integrated into the roll-up door. This meets fire code egress requirements while maintaining the functionality of the roll-up door.

This allows for the full opening to be utilized for RV access and also enhances the security of the unit, as it cannot be seen until the tenant opens the larger door.

This is especially beneficial during bad weather. Another alternative is the use of motorized doors for larger RV units.

However, a common challenge with this type of door is determining where to place the motor. To overcome this, Janus International has created the "Gliderol Operator Drive Unit," which houses an orbiting drive motor within the door coil and is suitable for continuous sheet curtain doors, making it ideal for RV and boat storage. U.S. Door & Building Components has also contributed to finding a solution, collaborating with LiftMaster to develop a compact motor operator that can be mounted inside the unit.

They now produce a small bracket specifically designed for this purpose, which comes with a radio control remote transmitter for easy door operation.

Additionally, a keypad can be mounted on the outside for added convenience. The cost for this solution is approximately $600, not including the cost of an electrician for installation.

Angled Parking:

What issue does the implementation of angled parking address? A non-right-angle entrance offers better accessibility compared to a 90-degree turn.

A 60-degree angle provides even smoother entry and exit, while also simplifying backing out.

However, angled parking requires wider doors, typically 14 feet in width, which can be more costly.

Can angled parking be used for RV storage? Yes, but it requires a pricier chain-hoisted commercial roll-up door instead of sectional doors.

Despite the higher construction costs, the benefits include using less land per unit and higher customer satisfaction. This design is less land-intensive than straight-in parking. Traditional straight-in parking lots require wider driveways of 60 to 90 feet to accommodate turning room for customers.

In contrast, using the standard 60-degree angle for angled parking reduces the driveway width to just 35 feet.

However, this also leads to increased land and construction costs. Is it cost-effective? Further research is needed to determine that. The same applies to covered parking structures; reducing the driveway width to 35 feet can lead to significant savings in land costs and increased rentable square footage.

While the initial construction costs for angled parking structures may be higher, it allows for more accessible parking spaces on the same plot of land compared to straight-in parking.

This is especially beneficial for RV and boat storage, where up to 50 spaces can be planned per acre, making it a more profitable use of land compared to the traditional 30 spaces per acre.

RV and boat storage in the form of condominium-style units is quickly becoming a lucrative trend in the industry. The focus is primarily on RVs, as their ownership rates have skyrocketed in recent years, especially among Baby Boomers.

In fact, studies have shown that one out of every twelve families who own a vehicle also has an RV.

While boat ownership has remained steady, the demand for RV storage continues to grow. This is in part due to stricter regulations on parking in residential areas, making the need for off-site storage essential.

As a result, there is a significant gap between the demand for storage and the available options, making this market more viable than ever before. However, the feasibility of vehicle storage does come with its challenges, such as high land costs, zoning restrictions, and finding the ideal location.

While some planned communities may offer storage options for RV and boat owners, this is not a common occurrence. This presents an opportunity to market these units as an extension of their homes, catering to their social nature and desire to be among like-minded individuals.

As a result, a condominium-style storage facility may catch their attention. The construction of a condominium-style storage facility may come with higher expenses, but customers seem willing to pay a premium for the convenience and security it offers.

These Facilities Can Include One or All These:

There are numerous options to consider offering:

Clubhouse

Lighting

Garage door openers

Complimentary motion detectors

Restrooms/showers

Dump stations (tap into the city's storm sewer or an on-site waste tank depending on the city's requirements)

Dog run

Lap pool

Weight room

Shelving in units

Playground

Wash bay

RV repair/tool rentals

Marina delivery

One huge room for indoor RV and boat storage

Winterization service

Seasonable RV parking

Lounge area with a computer for the seasonable RV owner

A unique café (even non-customers frequent these types of eating establishments)

Ice machines

Electricity in units

Propane

Air compressor

Pre-trip make ready (you can offer different levels of service).

The options are limited only by your educated imagination. In choosing which features to build, ensure that your insurance policy keeps up with these additional amenities.

Service Levels:

In order to provide a luxurious experience similar to a high-end golf clubhouse, it is important to offer both basic and advanced services to customers.

For example, a platinum membership could include all services such as fuel filling, boat towing to a convenient location, ice chest preparation, and standard battery charging.

Additionally, if the facility is near a lake, customers could also have the option of having their boat delivered or picked up from a dock for their convenience.

Other services that could be provided include RV cleaning, valet service, individual door alarms, video surveillance, and access to the facility's website for customers to monitor their units.

While these services are available to all customers, they are typically more appealing to those who own their units. Most customers value the security and convenience that come with ownership, making it a necessary aspect for long-term satisfaction.

Furthermore, it is crucial to offer 24/7 access to the facility. The monthly fees for these additional services could range from $40 to $70, depending on the level of service chosen by the customer.

It is recommended to gather feedback from customers during the initial opening of the facility to determine the value they place on these different levels of service. By offering a variety of service levels, it not only enhances the customer's experience but also helps foster a long-lasting relationship with them.

Creating a Distinctive Marketing Plan:

Captivate the interest of RV and boat owners by highlighting your unique services prior to advertising in the market. If you rely on word-of-mouth promotion, ensure accuracy by providing correct information about location, amenities, and pricing.

You must entice individuals to choose your storage facility by showcasing how it fulfills the needs of a specific buyer and excels at what it does.

Emphasize that your facility offers top-notch indoor and covered storage options for RVs and boats. Utilize all your selling points such as air conditioning, lighting, cleanliness, competitive prices, secure computerized gates, and monthly pest control to demonstrate the benefits of choosing your facility.

Visit nearby RV dealerships and consult with them about the requirements of RV owners. Leave them with flyers and treat their salespeople, managers, and owners to a meal. Offer them coupons for a complimentary tour and RV wash, along with lunch at your specialty café. Attending RV shows and hire a multimedia company to create a professional presentation.

The main dilemma is determining the appropriate price for these storage units. The RV storage industry lacks a standard model for this region. Fees vary based on the market and what it can yield.

Factors such as size, type, and additional features must be considered when setting the price. Consider climate control, open or canopy-covered options, indoor or self-parking, valet services, and electricity when establishing your pricing structure.

Possible rephrased text:

Effective strategies for maximizing profit in the RV and boat storage industry include offering various rates and "unit selling purchase prices" to gauge market demand.

Demographics also play a significant role, with Florida having higher prices compared to Arizona. It is crucial to conduct research by visiting existing storage facilities and studying their waiting lists and service charges.

Ultimately, supply and demand are the determining factors. Another approach is to gradually increase prices as occupancy levels rise. It is essential to consider the number of RV and boat owners in the area and the availability and convenience of storage facilities.

In the past, self-storage facilities used RV and boat storage as a supplemental source of income. However, the trend is shifting towards these facilities being developed as real estate investments, with ownership options similar to condominiums.

As a result, many entrepreneurs are drawn to this market, leading to its rapid growth in recent years. The concept of owning instead of leasing a storage unit for boats or RVs is gaining popularity due to the potential for a quick turnaround and profit, similar to real estate investments.

Developers appreciate the opportunity to continue building and selling units as they are quickly purchased. Therefore, when considering this type of storage, it is crucial to keep in mind the location and availability of land.

Unit owners also have the option to hold onto their units for a period and then customize and sell them for a significant profit. Some facility operators have even started providing financing for these units, creating another avenue for profit.

The only downside for facility owners is the lack of residual income from these sales. However, for customers, owning these units is like adding an extension to their home and business, providing a secure and convenient place to store their prized possessions, whether it be an RV or a luxury vehicle.

With the increasing number of RV owners seeking storage solutions, this trend is one that should not be overlooked.

Do you recall that the location of a storage facility is not as crucial as ensuring the security of one's investment? These lessees will inevitably discover your establishment.

While these types of facilities are exceptional, they require a considerable amount of time from conception to completion.

Therefore, it is imperative to sell the idea to the city, which can be particularly challenging due to its novelty. Remember, the city would much rather have a storage facility as a solution instead of RV owners parking in residential areas.

Persuade the prospective tenant to consider the option of purchasing instead of renting. This requires careful planning and an innovative approach towards presenting the concept to the tenant.

Before initiating the conversation, put yourself in the renter's shoes and ask yourself the same questions they will most likely ask: Why should I buy? What are the benefits? What price am I willing to pay?

Familiarize Yourself with Your Target Client:

It is crucial to establish a thorough understanding and strategy for what you will provide in terms of specialty storage.

These affluent individuals, who are often owners of luxurious recreational vehicles, value community and social connections and boast impressive financial portfolios.

For instance, some RVs, like the extravagant Prevost, can cost upwards of a million dollars, and their owners seek a dependable and secure facility to store their valuable investment. This is where your facility can come into play.

Cater to this demographic and word will spread about your exceptional offerings. All of these factors are essential to consider during the feasibility process, as your location, amenities, business plan, and pricing structure must align with their needs.

While community placement is not mandatory, the facility should have quick access to highways.

Furthermore, all amenities and security measures must be of the highest quality. RV owners also prefer paved surfaces over gravel, wider driveways, and enclosed storage options.

Ultimately, they seek convenience and simplicity and are willing to pay for it. When it comes to the facility's physical location, the safety of the asset is sometimes overshadowed by the accessibility to major highways.

Adequate research is essential.

Once you have conducted thorough research, you will realize that securing a loan for this type of venture differs greatly from obtaining one for a traditional self-storage facility. It is crucial to have a strong rapport with your bank/banker and a proven track record for successful financing.

Explore the market for other condominium-style RV and boat storage facilities. Even if it means traveling to a different state, educate yourself on their success stories, gather visual evidence, and include it in your loan application package for your bank.

Convince them that the time is now, and you are the one capable of making this a reality in this particular area. Keep in mind that this area has been witnessing development for a few years, so your banker may already be familiar with this type of facility.

Also, keep in mind that your land cost can be significantly lower since the facility does not have to be located in a prime corner. As mentioned earlier, your potential customers will eventually find you.

Analyze your project's economic viability and ensure that the rental rates will generate sufficient revenue to cover the land and construction expenses. Is the area already oversaturated, or is there still space for your RV and boat storage facility?

Will the zoning regulations pose a significant obstacle, or does the city recognize this as a solution for parking these large vehicles? Remember, banks base their loans on two crucial factors: economics and the market.

Thoroughly evaluate every opportunity as the lender will expect a comprehensive site review.

CHAPTER 4

STRATEGIES

The self-storage industry has undergone a gradual transformation, spurred by fierce competition and overdevelopment in certain regions.

This emphasizes the importance of thorough research and strategic planning for those aspiring to enter this field.

When devising your strategy, consider various factors such as the size of your facility, potential for expansion, and potential for specialization in certain areas.

Understanding the market and studying your competitors are crucial steps in this process. Additionally, it may be wise to resist the traditional layout of narrow aisles and rows of doors, and instead opt for larger buildings with maximum unit capacity.

This approach will not only set you apart from the competition but also ensure a successful and sustainable facility.

When is the Right Time to Expand? Instead of waiting until your facility is fully occupied, consider expanding when you have reached a stable occupancy level. It is beneficial to have a plan in place for expansion before your occupancy reaches 80 percent. In fact, when you have reached 65 percent occupancy, it is the opportune time to start expanding. If your facility is filling up faster than anticipated, it may be wise to begin expanding when you have reached 50 percent capacity.

Keep in mind that certain unit sizes may be more popular, providing a prime opportunity for expansion. If your facility is not limited by space, consider adding value by offering additional services such as mailbox and package drop-off and mailing services.

This can be done during the planning stages of your facility or even after it is fully occupied. Another factor to consider is the ability to modify your space to meet market demands. For example, if one particular unit size is in high demand, you can build walls and add doors to create more units of that size.

Additionally, if your facility's design allows, you can add insulation, heating, air conditioning, and dehumidification systems to offer climate-controlled units at a higher rate. When designing and constructing a new facility, it is important to keep in mind the potential for competition in the future.

This is why adding value is crucial to staying ahead of other facilities. Remember, offering climate control can give your facility an advantage over older facilities that do not provide this benefit. Do not neglect the maintenance of your property and try to improve it annually.

A well-maintained and valuable property will catch the attention of potential buyers and renters. Who knows, you may receive an offer that you cannot refuse in the future.

In the ever-evolving self-storage industry, we witness shifts in trends that elevate the standards of design, sophistication, and modernization.

These advancements are becoming increasingly common, with the inclusion of value-added services. Some examples of these services are multi-story buildings, conversions, multi-family buildings, condominium-style RV and boat storage options that offer ownership.

Offering complementary retail products and secondary services to both residential and commercial clients can lead to higher profits. Such services include truck rentals and packaging solutions, which are in high demand.

More than 60 percent of self-storage facilities now offer additional services, a significant increase from just 50 percent in the year 2001. To attract customers and maintain high occupancy rates, these facilities require heavy initial marketing efforts and positive word-of-mouth. The Army and Air Force Exchange Service (AAFES) are exploring the development of on-base self-storage or portable storage facilities at key locations throughout the United States.

This is not the first time they have considered this possibility. If you are looking to establish a storage facility near a military base, this could be a promising opportunity. Guidelines for Avoiding Common Mistakes in the Self-Storage Business.

Running a successful self-storage business requires a personal touch. Managing everything remotely can be challenging, but the most significant obstacle is often competition that overbuilds due to lack of knowledge or impulsive decisions.

Being overly aggressive and rushing without proper research can result in reduced profitability and resale potential.

Another common mistake is not seizing opportunities for growth when they arise. It is essential to act when the time is right and expand your business. Some of the crucial factors for achieving success in the self-storage industry include accurately assessing demand, adopting a realistic approach to financing, creating a viable pro forma, constructing a suitable facility, carefully pre-marketing, hiring competent staff, and having a clear exit strategy from the beginning.

These elements are vital for long-term success in the industry.

During your feasibility analysis, it is crucial to consider the land you own in a region where counties are adjacent.

This is significant because if you buy land and commence construction, you may find that someone else is developing a facility just one mile away in another county.

When it comes to securing funds, selecting an unsuitable equity partner can be a grave error. Smaller investors in self-storage often turn to friends and family, while larger ones opt for institutions or individuals with substantial assets. It is imperative to share the same values and beliefs with your equity partner. Be mindful not to solely focus on maximizing land use, neglecting the convenience of your customers.

Remember to establish an exit plan beforehand and refrain from over-promoting your facility with grandiose claims that you cannot fulfill. Unless you are constructing a condominium-style RV and boat storage facility, distributing flyers beyond a five-mile radius is fruitless.

Don't overlook the inclusion of special offers in your mailers and advertisements, which can help track the effectiveness of your marketing strategies. Promptly address any concerns or complaints from tenants, as failing to do so can lead to negative word-of-mouth and damage your reputation. Avoid being defensive or making excuses, and instead, handle the issue professionally. It is crucial to perform daily, routine maintenance and not let things slip through the cracks.

Allocate funds for annual capital improvements and do not wait until the last minute to solicit bids for services such as snow removal, lawn maintenance, and other necessary tasks. It is also essential to conduct background checks on all bidders to ensure credibility and quality of work.

CHAPTER 5

FEASIBILITY STUDY AND SITE SELECTION

Conducting a feasibility analysis and selecting an appropriate location are crucial steps in turning a vision into reality.

The process of constructing a self-storage facility is an exhilarating opportunity. Gaining knowledge about the industry, studying the market, securing financing, and visualizing the potential of your new enterprise is immensely satisfying.

While self-storage may seem like a straightforward concept, developing a successful facility requires meticulous planning, extensive research, and often, prior experience. When the time comes to acquire a site, swift action is necessary.

Should I Consider Hiring a Consultant From the Start? A reliable consultant has the ability to prevent numerous headaches and save you a significant amount of money in the long run. It is crucial to carefully review their experience and market knowledge and obtain references before deciding.

Consulting experts specialize in various stages of the business cycle, so it is important to identify the specific challenge and seek appropriate assistance. Some consultants may also offer feasibility assessments or other forms of consulting services.

Typically, consulting services are sought at the initial phases of a project, especially when it comes to building a self-storage facility.

However, it is essential to keep in mind that consultants have varying fee structures, with some charging hourly rates of $200 to $300, while others may offer a flat rate for the entire project which can be as high as $8,000 or more.

It is crucial to feel comfortable with the consultant you choose to work with, and this can be determined through a comprehensive conversation about the process. If they possess excellent communication skills and demonstrate confidence in their knowledge, it could be a good fit.

Additionally, if the consultant will be assisting with interactions with the city council, they must possess articulate and skillful communication abilities. To avoid complicated and overwhelming contracts, it is important to have a clear understanding of the fees, services provided, and expected timeframe outlined in the document.

Consulting services can be found through various sources such as national publications, the internet, trade associations, and trade shows, but most often through referrals. It is recommended to have a thorough conversation with at least one of their references to ensure that the consultant is capable of adequately supporting your needs.

Feasibility studies are essential in determining the suitability of investing in a self-storage business. This process will guide you towards either a successful venture or a clear warning that this may not be the right business for you.

Key inquiries to consider include:

Is the selected site feasible? Will it require an extensive amount of effort to transform it into a profitable self-storage location? What potential challenges must be overcome to convert this property into a profitable asset?

Furthermore, it is crucial to ensure that your facility not only has curb appeal but also integrates well within the community. For instance, if the area is predominantly filled with condos, your facility should mirror that aesthetic.

Unlike in the past, when the high demand for self-storage made research less critical, the industry now requires thorough evaluation.

Therefore, conducting a feasibility study is crucial in determining the viability of your project. This study encompasses several key areas such as the proposed site, market analysis, demographics, competition, design, demand, zoning, and financial projections.

By carefully analyzing this information, you can confidently make the decision to proceed with the project or walk away. It is essential to keep in mind that feasibility studies have their limitations, and it is crucial to maintain perspective and ask questions during the process.

For instance, the demand for self-storage differs across regions, with the Eastern part of the United States requiring less space compared to the West.

Therefore, it is vital to conduct thorough research and gather all necessary information to support your decision. One useful tool in determining the value of the land is the 2/3 rule, where the average rental rates per square foot of a 10'x15' and a 10'x10' space is multiplied by two-thirds.

This calculation provides a solid foundation for determining the maximum amount you should pay for the land on a per square foot basis.

<u>Location is a critical factor in the success of a self-storage facility</u>, and it is crucial to identify areas with a strong population base and signs of growth. It is also essential to personally inspect all the existing self-storage facilities in the vicinity, posing as a potential renter or a mystery shopper. This hands-on approach will provide valuable insight into the competition and potential demand for your facility.

Explore these properties as if you were a secret agent, and they were your adversaries. Be exceptionally polite and search for strategic enhancements. Assess their level of security and the availability of climate control. Identify their weaknesses and determine their occupancy levels.

Examine the surrounding streets and highways near the potential property. Obtain a traffic count, aiming for a high volume of around 20,000 cars within 24 hours. The state and city planning departments can assist in obtaining these statistics.

Evaluate the ease of access to the property. While the building must meet code requirements, the average unit size should be between 105 to 125 square feet. Sixty percent of the building should consist of units that are 10'x10' or smaller.

Consider maximizing space while also incorporating landscaping, functionality, and curb appeal. Let this feasibility study serve as your guide, rather than simply catering to the lender's expectations.

The financial viability should be demonstrated in a conservative and realistic manner, by an impartial third party.

If the proposed site can withstand thorough analysis, projections, and lease-up rates, then it has a greater potential for success. We can explore various markets, such as:

- This market has a lower-than-average demand for self-storage. Homeowners in this area may have enough space for a shed or barn, as zoning requirements are less stringent.

- Rural areas make up the majority of self-storage renters. They value easy access and see the facility as an extension of their home. They also appreciate added benefits, such as free move-in trucks, convenience, and a close proximity (3-5 miles) to their residence.

- Urban areas have heavy traffic patterns and potential obstacles to easy travel. However, these renters are not as concerned with location or tight drives, as long as the facility is within three miles.

- These renters are primarily businesses located in or near downtown. They may not mind smaller unit sizes, as their storage needs are typically smaller. Don't overlook demographic trends. Do your research and stay informed about the local market. Consult with the chamber of commerce, real estate firms, local publications, and newspapers. A helpful resource for information is Claritas, available at www.sitereports.com.

The Metropolitan Downtown Markets utilize a mathematical equation to estimate the demand for square footage. By multiplying the population within a five-mile radius by the demand factor of 3.5 square feet per person, you can determine the range of needed square footage. However, it is important to use your own judgement and not rely solely on this formula, as it may not always be accurate.

When considering purchasing a property, it is crucial to check the zoning regulations at City Hall rather than trusting the seller's word. If rezoning is necessary, it is up to you to decide if the cost and stress of involving attorneys, architects, and engineers is worth it.

Even if the property is already zoned correctly, it is advisable to communicate your plans with the neighbors through community meetings or open houses. This allows for transparency and organization when presenting your ideas.

A Phase 1 Environmental Assessment should also be conducted, and you can negotiate this cost with the seller. If the seller covers the expense, the results will remain confidential.

However, if negotiations fail, it is important to inform the seller that you will cover the cost, but the results will be made public.

This could potentially affect their selling plans if the assessment reveals any issues. It is worth noting that the majority of tenants have month-to-month leases, making it easier for landlords to consistently increase rent rather than waiting for leases to expire.

These tenants typically stay for an average of 14 months, allowing for quick adjustments to rental rates in response to market conditions. With this approach, landlords can continue to adapt to changing market demands by increasing rent for new tenants and twice-yearly for existing tenants.

Understanding Land Use Entitlements:

Before proceeding too far with a land purchase contract, it is crucial to have a thorough understanding of the land development permit process. This includes being aware of the local governmental agency's land use policies and whether they allow for the construction of a self-storage facility on the chosen site.

Deciphering Entitlements:

A land use entitlement grants a land developer the authority to develop a property as per the submitted plans. All municipalities have their own set of land use policies that dictate the development of a community. Generally, privately-owned land falls into three main categories: residential, commercial, and industrial. These categories collectively form a community's "general plan," and each individual parcel of land is categorized into specific "zones" to outline the permissible land uses.

Therefore, it is essential to determine if a proposed self-storage facility aligns with the general plan and zoning designations.

Development Process:

The project's architect and civil engineer must collaborate to prepare a comprehensive design for the proposed self-storage facility. This is the first step in initiating a land use submission.

Permitted Use without Discretionary Review:

Compliance with the jurisdiction's zoning ordinance, including site-specific development standards, is mandatory.

This section covers various development standards, such as maximum allowable building size, lot coverage by buildings, building setbacks from property lines, maximum building heights, required parking, driveway widths, and landscape site coverage.

These factors heavily influence the project's design and are generally reviewed at a staff level in an informal process, bypassing the political process and simplifying the approval process. In some cases, self-storage projects may be permitted in less desirable industrial or commercial zones without the need for a discretionary review process.

Permitted Use with Discretionary Review:

In this area, self-storage is allowed by default; however, obtaining a project entitlement requires a discretionary evaluation of the project's layout.

This entails a "site plan review" or "design reviews" by the agency. This process grants the agency the authority to modify or alter the design elements, such as colors, shapes, and details. It can add complexity to the approval process. One or more individuals may complete this procedure informally, or a formal public hearing may be held by a board.

The goal is to give the jurisdiction more say in the project's design. Although approval is highly likely, the process may take up to four months to complete.

Many self-storage projects fall under this category.

Conditional Use:

Although more intricate, self-storage is no longer permitted by default. The onus is on the development team to demonstrate the suitability of self-storage for the proposed property. This conditional use permit process involves a thorough examination of the project's design.

Here, the required design standards are significantly higher. Final approval is granted through a public hearing.

The chances of approval are high if the project meets three main criteria:

1. Adherence to the zone's development standards as per the zoning ordinance.
2. Sensible integration into the surrounding community, particularly if residential properties are nearby.
3. High-quality aesthetics in the building design and landscaping.

These are the areas where most self-storage projects face scrutiny, and it typically takes three to six months for approval. Rezone or Zone Change:

If self-storage is not allowed in a specific zone, the zoning of the parcel may need to be altered. This "re-zoning" process is complex and, once again, the development team must provide sufficient evidence. It involves a high level of scrutiny by the jurisdiction. Final approval is granted through a public hearing, and the process can take up to nine months.

Plan Revision: In certain situations, the property may fall under a general plan category that prohibits the establishment of self-storage facilities.

This could be due to the area being designated for residential, commercial, or open space development, thus disallowing storage as a viable land use.

However, as self-storage is often mistakenly classified as industrial land usage, a revision of the general plan may be necessary for obtaining approvals, which could take up to a year.

Understanding Construction Codes:

For years, developers and other professionals in the building industry have been frustrated by the lack of uniformity in construction codes across the United States.

This inconsistency leads to varying requirements for the design and construction of self-storage projects in different regions of the country.

Fortunately, efforts are now being made to improve code uniformity. These efforts have resulted in the creation of the International Code Council (ICC), which is made up of members from the Building Officials Code Administrators International (BOCA), Southern Building Code Congress

International (SBCCI), and International Conference of Building Officials (ICBO).

The ICC has developed a new comprehensive code, known as the International Building Code (IBC), which aims to be the unified code for the entire country.

This code, completed in 1997, is currently being adopted by most states, and its implementation should eliminate discrepancies in construction standards for self-storage facilities.

However, a challenge remains as some larger cities have their own local codes, which may not be covered by the IBC. These local codes can be modified by local authorities, resulting in a multitude of considerations. Nevertheless, the IBC sets forth the requirements for all buildings, including self-storage facilities.

Classification and Definition of Occupancy: According to the current self-storage code, a "self-storage facility" is defined as real property specifically designed for the rental or leasing of individual storage spaces, where customers can store and remove their personal belongings on a self-service basis.

This type of self-storage is categorized as "Storage Group S." Group S-1 is intended for storing items with moderate hazards, while Group S-2 is intended for items with low hazards.

Architects typically use the S-2 classification, but the final decision rests with the local building officials.

Classification of Construction Types:

There are five types of construction, classified based on the materials used. These are:

- Type Uses non-combustible materials and is typically used for taller structures over four stories.

- Type II: Uses non-combustible materials such as concrete, masonry, and steel, and is suitable for smaller buildings of four stories or less. Type II is less restrictive than Type I and is often seen in larger self-storage projects.

- Type III: Uses non-combustible or fire-resistant exterior materials, with non-fire-rated interior materials. This category includes self-storage facilities of medium and small sizes. It also allows for non-combustible exterior materials but permits heavy timber for the interior.

- Type IV: Rarely used in self-storage buildings.

- Type V: Allows for all materials permitted by the code, except for wood-framed buildings for storage purposes.

Construction Types I, II, III, and V can also be further classified as sub-type 'A' or 'B', with sub-type 'A' requiring higher levels of fire resistance.

The International Building Code (IBC) has set general guidelines for the maximum number of stories allowed for each construction type, which are:

- Five stories for Type II-A construction

- Four stories for Type II-B construction

- Four stories for Type III-A and III-B construction In some cases, the number of stories may be increased if automatic fire sprinkler systems are installed.

The maximum allowable floor areas for these construction types are: - 39,000 square feet for Type II-A - 26,000 square feet for Type II-B - 39,000 square feet for Type III-A - 26,000 square feet for Type III-B Self-storage projects fall under this category of construction types.

The occupant load determines the usual number of people in a building and mandates the presence of safe exits.

According to the IBC, warehouses must have an occupant load of one person per 500 square feet of gross building area. Once this has been established, emergency exits must be designed to facilitate a smooth evacuation from fire-threatened areas. After the exits are in place, a clear pathway must be provided for safe passage to these areas.

Hallways with a capacity of over 30 occupants must have a one-hour fire rating, making them corridors.

However, if the building has sprinklers, this fire rating is not necessary for hallways with 30 or more occupants. Exit requirements include specifications for minimum hallway widths, heights, exit door sizes, door swing direction, stair tread width, stair riser height, and stair landing sizes.

The IBC also outlines guidelines for fire rating corridors and individual building components. Exterior walls must have a fire rating based on the overall construction type of the building and their proximity to property lines.

Walls within 10 feet of the property line must have a one-hour fire rating. In certain cases, corridors and stairwell walls may require a two-hour fire rating for buildings with four or more stories, or a one-hour fire rating for buildings with three or less.

Floor construction and ceilings below must also have a fire rating like interior walls. To prevent the spread of fire between floors, vertical shafts between floors must have a one or two-hour fire rating. Mechanical room walls must be constructed with a one-hour fire rating. The IBC also includes accessibility requirements for people with physical disabilities. It also covers engineering-related elements such as wind resistance, earthquake resistance, weight resistance, and building material performance standards.

Twenty-nine states have adopted the IBC, demonstrating its widespread acceptance and implementation across the country.

Determining the Site Layout and Unit Mix:

Choosing the optimal site layout and unit mix for a self-storage project is a critical decision that can significantly impact the success of the facility. It is essential to carefully consider this aspect as it can affect the initial lease-up process and ultimately, the bottom line.

Therefore, it is crucial to have a long-term strategy in mind when designing the unit mix, aiming to maximize income and ensure a quick lease-up rate.

While some facilities have opted for a one-size-fits-all approach, such as a facility in New Jersey with 500-plus units that built all 5'x10's, or one in Texas with 400 10'x20's units, they have since expanded their unit mix due to customer demand. This highlights the importance of strategic planning and avoiding the mistake of having all units of the same size.

To determine the ideal unit mix, it is vital to analyze the area's demographics by researching and contacting existing facilities to understand the storage size demand.

A recommended guide is to have 20% of 5'x10's, 10% of 10'x20's, 25% of 10'x15's, 40% of 10'x20's, and 5% of 10'x25's. Additionally, incorporating some 5'x5's as low-cost "leaders" can be beneficial.

Overall, it is advisable to have a range of unit sizes between 90 and 130 square feet, avoiding an oversaturation of large units. While it may take longer to rent smaller units, the income generated per square footage is significantly higher compared to a single large unit.

This mix can also work well for climate-controlled units, which should be considered in the facility. If the project is being constructed in phases, it is advantageous to start with the most popular unit size and plan the unfinished part accordingly.

Planning Your Site Layout:

Several factors must be considered when planning the site layout for a self-storage facility. These include the size, shape, and terrain of the land, any initial challenges with the land, and zoning regulations. Additionally, there may be setbacks or easements required by the city, such as landscape buffers, as well as considerations for sanitary sewers, drain fields, and storm drains.

It is also crucial to evaluate the proximity of the site to environmentally protected areas, such as rivers, creeks, or designated wetlands, and avoid building on parcels with environmental corridors that must be maintained according to specific guidelines.

To ensure a successful site layout, it is essential to consult with a qualified architect and engineer familiar with self-storage development. Their expertise can prevent costly mistakes and determine the maximum buildable area and rentable square footage of the site.

When making decisions for your facility, it is important to consider factors such as the type of facility (single or multi-story), climate-controlled units, and any specialty storage options.

Your goal is to maximize usable space without sacrificing functionality. Other factors to consider when planning the layout of your site include the design of the buildings, their location, and whether they will have interior or exterior access, as well as one or two-sided doors.

These decisions may also be influenced by property lines. It is crucial to carefully determine the entry and exit points of your facility in order to ensure efficient flow and security. Seeking professional advice and researching popular unit sizes and amenities, such as climate-controlled units, can also aid in making informed decisions.

If your target market includes businesses, it may be wise to offer larger units and consider incorporating "flex space technology" for resizing options. While there are architects who specialize in self-storage design, most developers must make critical decisions on their own.

Attending conventions and speaking with experienced developers can provide valuable insights and help avoid common mistakes. Additionally, conducting a feasibility study and carefully selecting a site that aligns with your goals and potential exit strategy can greatly impact the success of your self-storage project.

Ultimately, a highly visible site within a populated area is likely to perform well and retain higher value over time, making it worth investing in slightly more expensive land with good visibility. Ideally, the best site for a self-storage facility would be one that is already zoned for self-storage use.

The task of selecting a site for a new self-storage facility is a challenging one, as it involves weighing the pros and cons. Various factors such as land cost, demographics, zoning, development potential, population density, and visibility must be considered. The chosen location must also be feasible and support the addition of storage space.

Ideally, the site should be situated on a major road or travel route with a daily traffic volume of 20-30 thousand cars.

According to Mini-Storage Messenger, there are four types of sites that are typically preferred.

The first is highly visible and contiguous, meaning it is easily seen from highways and surface streets and serves the population center.

The second type is marginally visible and contiguous, with most of the site hidden behind other retail or development uses.

The third type is contiguous but not readily visible, often located in a cul-de-sac, warehouse development, or other area where drive-by visibility is low.

The fourth type is non-contiguous, located away from the population center and may or may not be visible from travel corridors.

All these factors must be taken into consideration when deciding. While less contiguous sites may be cheaper, they require more investment in marketing. The ideal size for a storage facility is 2.5 to 3.5 acres, and satellite sites in close proximity can also be a convenient option.

Zoning plays a critical role in determining a suitable site. It is best to choose a location that is zoned for self-storage as a "use by right." Seeking special use permits or zoning variances can be risky, time-consuming, and expensive.

However, if one is familiar with the local politics and understands the entitlement process, it may be worth investing in. Some sites may pose more challenges than they are worth and may not be suitable for self-storage development.

This can be due to various issues such as easements, soil problems, retention requirements, wetlands, toxic waste, contamination, impact fees, improvement districts, traffic mitigation fees, or assessments. It is crucial to thoroughly assess these factors before finalizing a site.

Carefully assess the expenses and obstacles once you have completed your research. This will enable you to evaluate all potential locations, even those with difficulties.

Additional Considerations for Choosing a Site:

Shape of the land and quality of the soil Demographics of the surrounding area Zoning regulations Population density Likelihood of other self-storage developers building nearby in the future Any easements, retention requirements, or impact fees associated with the site Presence of wetlands or hazardous materials Fees for mitigating traffic impact Remember: seek out a property situated on a major road or travel route. Aim for a minimum daily traffic count of 2,500 vehicles.

CHAPTER 6
THE LOAN PROCESS

Congratulations, you have discovered the perfect location for your new self-storage site. The demand is high, and the growth potential is promising. You have put in the necessary effort, attending seminars and trade shows, researching building designs and layouts, analyzing the competition, and obtaining the necessary zoning and approvals.

Now, the only thing left to do is find a lender who shares your vision and believes in your project. When approaching a lender for financing for a self-storage facility, the first question they will ask is if the market can support your proposed development. It is crucial to be well-prepared to answer this question in order to secure the loan.

The lender needs to have confidence in your assessment and a thorough understanding of your proposal. Therefore, it is important to thoroughly study and become an expert in the self-storage industry.

Don't be afraid to ask questions, such as how many self-storage applications the lender has reviewed in the past six months, the amount of capital allocated for self-storage loans, the qualifications of the lending firm, and the timeline for approval and closing.

Before approaching a lender, it is important to have a checklist of required documents, including a business plan, resume, personal and business tax returns, financial statements, site plans, budget, feasibility study, environmental survey, zoning and permits, and third-party contracts.

These documents should be presented to the lender in the form of a construction financing request, project overview, investor and developer qualifications, management qualifications, feasibility study, construction budget and timeline, and income and expense projections.

Additional information, suchfirmschitectural drawings, environmental studies, zoning and building information, and resumes for the construction and management firms, should also be included. It is important to keep your lender involved throughout the entire process. Surprises can cause delays and headaches for both parties, so it is best to have open communication and keep the lender updated on any changes or developments.

Understanding the evaluation process and the reasons behind a lender's analysis will help you assess the financing options for your project more realistically. In conclusion, securing a loan for a self-storage facility requires thorough preparation, expertise in the industry, and open communication with the lender. By following this approach, you can increase your chances of obtaining the necessary funding for your project.

A financial institution views a self-storage property through the same lens as its owner. Both seek to generate cash flow from the facility's operations to earn a return on their invested capital.

The lender's main goal is to recover the loan amount and earn interest on it, which is their rate of return or yield. However, there are significant disparities in how financial institutions and owners calculate and project cash flow.

Owners typically use the standard income and expense/cash flow projection, which includes potential rental income, vacancy and credit loss, gross collected rental income, and other sources of income like late fees and box sales. This is followed by the deduction of operating expenses to arrive at the Net Operating Income (NOI).

Depreciation is not included in this calculation. On the other hand, lenders have a different approach to projecting cash flow as it helps them determine the value of the self-storage facility. They add a separate expense category for professional management, which is not included in the owner's projection.

The difference in perspectives leads to a contrasting calculation of the facility's NOI, which is crucial for reaching a mutual understanding on the loan amount. Once the adjusted NOI is projected, lenders apply various methods to determine the property's value based on the first year's operating expenses, including management costs. Commercial real estate lenders primarily consider a property's ability to consistently generate cash flow above the required debt payments when making credit decisions.

Since self-storage properties have a month-to-month lease structure, it is essential to work with a lender who understands this unique aspect of the industry. Lenders tend to favor projects they are familiar with, and it may be necessary to educate them about the feasibility of self-storage projects and provide examples from across the country.

While many institutions are becoming more familiar with the industry, some still have limited knowledge. As a result, there are more options for capital in different forms, especially during the permanent financing stage after the construction or bridge loan term ends.

The Developer's Guide to Obtaining a Construction Loan: A developer must present a persuasive loan proposal to a lender, one that is so appealing that the lender will have confidence in the project's success and view it as a sound credit risk. It is crucial to include all aspects of the project in the financing request, which should be thoroughly evaluated and meticulously prepared.

Due to the limited number of construction lenders targeting the self-storage industry, the role of commercial mortgage brokers has become increasingly important in assisting self-storage developers, buyers, and owners in securing funding.

CHAPTER 7

PLANNING AND CONSTRUCTION

Information on Construction Pricing:

It is often said that what goes up, must come down. However, this may not hold true for construction costs. While metal buildings remain the most cost-effective option, incorporating alternative materials like composites, metal panels, and stucco has become necessary to reduce costs.

The use of energy-efficient electrical options is also being considered.

Roofing, particularly standing-seam metal roofing, continues to be the preferred choice for self-storage facilities.

This is not expected to change in the near future. However, the rising cost of steel has caused a ripple effect, leading to increased prices for concrete, drywall, paint, and other materials used between the outer and inner walls.

Insulation, in particular, has seen a shortage and a significant increase in price, affecting the construction of climate-controlled facilities. Despite these challenges, the self-storage industry is thriving.

It is essential, however, to prioritize quality when building a new facility to ensure a good return on investment.

Selecting a Contractor:

There are two alternatives for the development of your project: Do your research and find a skilled contractor.

Or undertake the role of a general contractor by coordinating with your own subcontractors, including suppliers and builders.

Taking on the responsibility of a contractor is time-consuming and entails a considerable amount of pressure.

Alternatively, you can engage a general contractor who will manage the entire project, but this will, of course, be a more costly path.

This is where a reliable supplier comes into play. In my opinion, the main distinction between a Steel Building Manufacturer and a Steel Building Supplier/Broker is that the Supplier/Broker is more attentive to clients' needs.

When it comes to self-storage, price is not the most significant factor. For instance, American Steel Buildings, Inc. conducts a large volume of business with several manufacturers, allowing them to secure lower prices than what the end user can obtain directly from the manufacturer. A reputable supplier employs construction crews that specialize in assembling self-storage buildings. These suppliers have great confidence in the crews they use, which can result in significant cost savings for you.

You will still need to arrange for your own concrete pouring, but the supplier will provide you with detailed plans outlining the process. Simply provide this requirement to your concrete contractors and let them handle it.

Be cautious about the suppliers you choose. Many may claim to manufacture buildings and promise to save you money. To be completely honest, a significant number of them are not being truthful. They use a phrase that implies they represent the manufacturer in order to get away with this claim. Select a national supplier that conducts a high volume of business with leading manufacturers.

This enables them to secure the best rates for you. The high volume of business these reputable suppliers have with various manufacturers puts them in a position to look out for your best interests. Furthermore, a dependable supplier will stay by your side throughout the entire project. While some manufacturers may do the same, most do not prioritize smaller projects as much as suppliers do.

As the owner or developer, you will need to have a close working relationship with the general contractor for an extended period of time. Therefore, it is crucial to conduct a thorough interview. When making your hiring decision, there are two key points to consider.

You and the general contractor should feel comfortable working together, and the general contractor should be capable of providing the necessary services.

Additionally, the supplier/broker conducts a significant volume of business with door and insulation manufacturers, which can result in cost savings for you. This also means that you will receive greater value in terms of both price and service.

Deciding on the Phasing of a Self-Storage Project:

Should you construct your facility in one go, or in stages? If you opt for a phased approach, it is crucial to design your project in a way that allows for a diverse range of units to ensure high occupancy at the time of its opening.

Once your feasibility study is complete and you have selected a suitable site, you can determine whether to undertake the entire project at once or in stages. This decision will largely be influenced by your financing options. Moreover, the amount you have borrowed upfront will also impact your choice as it can reduce your interest.

Additionally, the overall size of the project may also play a role in your decision-making process. Some lenders may prefer a phased approach. These considerations can also guide you in determining the unit mix. As your occupancy increases, you may want to add more units of a particular size that is in high demand. Adhering to the Americans with Disabilities Act (ADA): The Americans with Disabilities Act was passed in 1990, leading to significant changes in the construction industry.

Numerous regulations and requirements were implemented to make buildings more accessible to individuals with physical disabilities. The federal definition of a disability encompasses any person with a physical or mental limitation that significantly impacts one or more major daily activities.

This law applies to both new construction and major renovations, as a considerable portion of the population falls under its protection. In fact, 20% of non-institutionalized Americans above the age of 15 report having a disability that falls under the ADA category. It is crucial to enlist the services of professional architects and engineers who are well-versed in ADA regulations to determine the design requirements. Non-compliance with these regulations can result in significant penalties, sometimes amounting to thousands of dollars per day. While some of these regulations may be open to interpretation by state authorities, it is essential to strive for compliance from the outset.

For instance, this may involve providing a five-foot circle for wheelchair maneuvering and ensuring accessibility to toilets, handles, pulls, latches, locks, and other operating devices on accessible doors.

The design of door handles must allow for easy one-handed gripping, without requiring excessive force or wrist movements. The optimal mounting height for handles is no higher than 48 inches from the floor. Swinging doors should be able to be opened with a maximum force of six pounds, which is equivalent to the weight of a gallon of liquid.

Additionally, the slope of sidewalks leading to the facility should be no more than a quarter inch per foot for both asphalt and concrete surfaces. Collaborating proactively with building inspectors is recommended by experts to reach a mutual understanding on ADA requirements and ensure compliance with the city's interpretation of the code.

When preparing and constructing a facility, one crucial aspect to consider is lighting. It must be both aesthetically appealing at night and subdued during the night hours.

It is recommended to have lighting in units larger than 5X10, but caution must be taken with incandescent bulbs as they can potentially cause fires. For this reason, fluorescent fixtures are the safer option. Motion sensors should also be installed to activate lighting when a customer enters the service area, promoting energy efficiency.

Alternatively, a high-tech option is available where lights are activated based on a tenant's access code at the gate. For hallways, fluorescent lighting is preferred for its energy efficiency and low heat production.

As for exterior lighting, the industry standard is high-pressure sodium wall-pack units that are surface mounted on the building, providing efficient and pleasing illumination. Most exterior lighting circuits are controlled by photocells, automatically turning on at dusk and off at dawn.

Entry and exit keypads are commonly used to control the horizontal sliding gates in most self-storage facilities. Different options are available from vendors for these gates, but it is important to ensure that they are well-lit for customer convenience.

Customers should not have to leave their vehicles to use the gate system, and for those with RVs, installing a high and low-key pad can make the process even easier. Water access is a crucial aspect to consider during the construction phase.

Make sure to install hose bibs in various areas to facilitate cleaning and washing of driveways and roll-up doors, as well as for general cleaning tasks.

When building an apartment for living or for an employee, it is essential to provide heating and air conditioning for comfort. A common mistake in two-story designs is not installing a split system to maintain separate temperatures in the office and apartment. This can lead to discomfort for customers if the thermostat is in the apartment, as the office may become too cold.

Adding ceiling fans is a great way to enhance the ambiance of the office and apartments while maximizing energy efficiency for heating and cooling. Designing climate-controlled storage spaces can be challenging.

One mistake often made is climate controlling the upstairs of a two-story building to make it more appealing to customers. However, this is not efficient.

If possible, opt to cool the downstairs of the building instead. Effective insulation is crucial for energy efficiency, especially in heated spaces in colder climates. Another challenge is managing condensation caused by cooling humid air. This can be addressed by installing heated condensate drains, which evaporate the condensation and eliminate the need for piping it outside the building.

Consider installing air curtains between the doors to an exterior or staging area. These curtains, made of heavy-duty plastic sheets, help retain heated or cooled air inside the building while allowing customers to pass through quickly.

For roll-up doors, there are many vendors that offer affordable and tension-adjustable options with excellent hardware. Ensure to choose wisely and invest in quality doors for long-term satisfaction.

When designing a space, partitions are an important factor to consider. A highly effective design technique involves attaching partitions from the front to the back of the building first, and then cutting the tracks inside the building at the rear of the spaces.

This allows for future changes if the unit mix is not suitable. Recently, developers have shifted away from the traditional 5'x10' storage space layout and have begun to favor 10'x5' storage spaces. This not only makes the space more marketable with its wide, eight-foot-roll-up door, but it also works well for units located on a five-foot interior corridor.

Maneuvering a sofa into a 10'x5' space is much easier compared to a 5'x10' space. Roll-up doors are typically a better choice over swing doors. The cost difference is not significant, and roll-up doors do not intrude into corridors like swing doors do. In the current market, facility operators are incorporating attractive foyers or reception areas into their design plans.

An upscale hotel lobby can serve as a great inspiration for this. Bright decor, specialty lighting, treated concrete floors, and wider hallways are all elements that draw interest. Large storefront windows not only provide natural light but also give customers a sense of security.

Choosing the right tile, carpeting, and wall finishes can elevate your space into a showcase.

Choose granite counter tops as they are durable, timeless, and add a professional touch compared to Formica. Track lighting and recessed can-light fixtures can lend a sense of sophistication and design to your space. Avoid the mundane look of fluorescent fixtures in your business area.

Customers can appreciate the quality and professionalism of a beautifully designed space and feel more at ease when leasing from you.

Don't be afraid to use glass, fine wood, and metal to create a refined and elegant style. Consider consulting with a decorator to further enhance the presentation.

Each choice should have two customer contact areas - a high counter (40 to 42 inches) for quick and convenient payments, and a low counter (30 to 32 inches) for customers to sit at while initially renting the space. This design should also facilitate easy maintenance for employees, with equipment such as copiers, fax machines, and stackable trays located in a back area out of sight of customers.

A lounge area with an internet connection, fax machine, phone, and conference table can be a valuable addition. It is also important to have a mop sink and service sink nearby for regular cleaning purposes.

Lastly, a designated area with a sink, refrigerator, and microwave is essential for employees to have a space to eat away from customers.

As technology rapidly advances, top industry leaders are offering cutting-edge solutions for camera surveillance, access control, and door alarms. In place of metal siding, many buildings are now opting for more upscale exteriors such as brick or concrete masonry, steering away from the industrial aesthetic and incorporating elements like block, glazing, and glass.

If you are considering converting a multi-story building into a self-storage facility, it is crucial to understand the nuances of this type of construction versus starting from scratch, which is discussed in detail in chapter 3. It should be noted that the design of a self-storage building should not resemble a traditional block structure. Instead, incorporating variations in horizontal planes, materials, and proportions is key.

The use of color can also help break up the block-like appearance. Overall, modern self-storage facilities are becoming increasingly upscale compared to a decade ago, with a focus on appealing to the predominantly female renter demographic.

Security is also a top priority, as customers must feel safe and comfortable on the premises. Before beginning any self-storage project, it is essential to consider and satisfy the requirements of the community planning committee, as they hold the power to approve, request changes, or deny the project. In many urban areas, metal siding is no longer allowed, and instead, a more polished look using concrete, masonry, or stucco is preferred to blend in with the surrounding neighborhood.

Local review boards have also implemented oversight committees that impose strict architectural and landscape design standards, adding another layer of challenge for self-storage developers.

While the design and construction of self-storage facilities have evolved over time, the materials used have largely remained the same. Although some facilities may have been built with wood framing and drywall in the past, the predominant trend now is towards pre-engineered steel systems.

Additionally, the majority of self-storage buildings today are constructed with non-combustible materials, as per type II (IBC) regulations, with wood used only for framing.

This is due to the durability and sense of security that materials like steel and concrete provide. In essence, the three main materials used in self-storage construction remain steel, concrete, and masonry.

Eco-Friendly Construction:

Eco-Friendly Construction is a term used to describe the process of building a structure with minimal impact on the environment, prioritizing the health of its inhabitants and resource conservation throughout its lifespan.

By reducing human exposure to harmful materials and utilizing renewable resources, this approach aims to reduce energy consumption and consider the long-term environmental impact of the materials used. It also focuses on protecting and restoring the local environment, including air, water, soil, and plant life.

As a result, more self-storage owners are considering eco-friendly development not only for its benefits to the environment but also for potential tax advantages. To learn more about green buildings, you can visit websites such as www.buildinggreen.com, www.smartcommunities.ncat.org/buildings, and www.edcmag.com.

Ensuring Safety:

When customers use your self-storage property, they should feel at ease and confident in your property's security measures.

It is essential to plan for security requirements and systems during the early stages of your construction. Any additions or changes made later on can be costly. This includes considering the electrical supply wiring for low-voltage security systems, conduit and raceways for camera and alarm connections, gates and gate operators, and equipment closets for housing electronic components.

While your security vendor will provide specifications, be sure to communicate any additional requirements you may have.

It is also crucial to consider how you want tenants to use and access different areas of your property, as it will directly impact on the construction and security plan.

Breaking down the security system into separate subsystems for power, data, and physical installation can help visualize the construction requirements.

Additionally, implementing physical protection measures such as fences, walls, lights, and landscaping can contribute to crime prevention through environmental design (CPTED), which utilizes proper design and environment to reduce crime and create a perception of risk.

CPTED emphasizes the importance of utilizing architectural design and landscaping to ensure intruders are easily spotted and people on site are highly visible.

This includes incorporating prickly plants like bougainvillea and Natal plum along fence lines and walls. In terms of perimeter fencing at self-storage facilities, it is recommended to have a minimum height of eight feet, with tubular steel being a popular choice due to its increased strength.

Access control systems personnel and line of protection, limiting entry to only authorized tenants and personnel, and tracking their access time and specific areas.

Self-storage operators also have the option to restrict access for delinquent tenants in accordance with their contract and state lien laws. Entry to the facility is usually granted through a numeric keypad, but there are also magnetic card readers and combined keypads with magnetic readers available.

These systems are often integrated with electronic gates, management software, and individual door alarms if present. It is crucial to use high-security locks inside the facility, with disc locks being a favored choice by law enforcement professionals due to their resilience.

Cylinder locks are another option, embedded in a specially designed latch and providing over 10,000 keys differs with a seven-pin barrel keyway that cannot be easily cut. Individual door alarms are a growing trend, allowing for easy code changes when a customer vacates.

However, concerns about privacy arose when fingerprinting was introduced at a California facility. A survey revealed that very few tenants had any objections to it being a requirement in their lease, emphasizing the importance of not letting anyone slip through the security measures.

Identity theft is a growing criminal activity that now poses a threat to self-storage businesses. In response, the law has loosened restrictions on how personal identifiers are stored, used, and disposed of.

As a responsible business, it is crucial to safeguard your customers' information and comply with legal requirements, especially when conducting a lien sale.

Effective access control is essential for smooth day-to-day operations. It is important to have full control over property access and ensure safe and convenient traffic flow. Proper planning allows for the creation of a gated area, ample turn areas, and driveways that facilitate easy entry and exit.

Depending on the property layout, access may require a single gate or multiple gates for one-way traffic. Each gate operator needs power and Wi-Fi connectivity, and entry devices require a conduit to the gate operator location or primary office.

Roll-up doors at loading docks or drive-through areas can greatly enhance the appeal of a self-storage facility, particularly for commercial clients. It is important to consider factors such as access control, duration of door opening, and alarm systems when designing the construction plan.

The concept of remote management is making a comeback in the self-storage industry.

In the early days, potential customers would simply call a number, meet someone at the facility, make payment, and gain access. This approach may be suitable for rural communities as it eliminates the need for full-time employees and automatic access expenses.

Self-service kiosks are becoming increasingly popular among self-storage owners as a way to boost profitability.

Many industry leaders, including Public Storage, Shurgard, Storage Solutions, and SecurCare, have already implemented kiosks on their properties. This technology allows for 24/7 rental of units without the need for a facility manager.

Customers can take virtual tours of available units, select and pay for their chosen unit, purchase a lock, and print a rental agreement, all through the kiosk. This innovative solution may be beneficial for your facility as well.

This service offers existing customers the convenience of managing their accounts and making payments, all while reducing staffing costs.

With most kiosks equipped with a speakerphone, live customer service agents are just a call away to assist with any queries. The kiosk also provides a permanent "open" sign, potentially boosting profits.

In addition, security is taken care of with a fingerprint scanner, license reader, signature pad, and check reader. The kiosk also features a digital camera to verify new tenants and deter any potential wrongdoers. Furthermore, the kiosks can be integrated with SSA Counter Measures for real-time customer ID verification, credit scoring, bankruptcy screening, and criminal background checks.

Acting as a manager's assistant, the kiosk allows for more flexibility and potentially reduces working hours. This makes it a great option for semi-retired individuals seeking maximum convenience for themselves and their customers.

These outdoor computers offer various automated services, including a digital camera to capture and store photos of potential tenants, a speakerphone to connect with the manager or a call center for assistance, a fingerprint scanner to validate identity, and a driver's license scanner for photo and record storage.

They also provide real-time credit cards and check processing, along with background screening using county-level criminal records from all 50 states.

Security Systems: Security systems can be a key differentiator for your property, setting it apart from your competitors. Door alarms for individual units can be either wired or wireless, requiring similar power and data connections.

It is important to consider the placement of the alarm control and communication components for convenience. In some cases, unit alarm components can also serve as lighting controls, but this must be carefully planned with coordination between security vendors, electricians, and lighting contractors.

Your local authority may have specific requirements for alarm notifications, such as being terminated at a monitoring facility or the police station. They may also restrict the use of external sirens due to community or neighborhood considerations.

These factors should be considered when creating a security plan and incorporating it into construction plans. Video Surveillance: Closed circuit television (CCTV) has been proven to be an effective deterrent against theft and vandalism. The current generation of digital video recorders and surveillance systems offer advanced features and reliability, making them a valuable asset in protecting your property and providing excellent customer service.

Each camera requires a nearby power supply or connection to a central power supply in the equipment room. For longer distances, a larger coaxial cable may be necessary, which can take up more conduit space.

Some owners are choosing alternative technologies such as twisted pair wiring or fiber optic backbones for longer distances. Plenum-rated wiring may also be required for indoor structures.

Careful consideration should be given to the placement of cameras to provide evidence and limit liability. As the property owner, it is important to ensure that your investment is protected. High traffic areas, entrances, elevator lobbies, and loading areas should all be covered by surveillance.

The Choice is Yours:

When it comes to security systems, there are numerous solutions with varying features. It is important to keep in mind that everyone becomes an expert when it comes to spending money. Look for reputable security providers who specialize in self-storage.

Consider their tenure in the industry, ask about their history and references in your area. It is crucial to choose a supplier who will be able to support you for years to come.

Sound systems and intercoms are important features in a self-storage facility that can help alleviate customer anxiety caused by the large walls. Not only does the addition of piped-in music create a calming atmosphere, but it also serves as a public address system that requires proper planning and preparation.

This may involve pre-planning for transit locations through firewalls and ensuring that the wiring is clearly outlined in construction plans. By providing intercom call buttons at key locations throughout the property, customers can easily communicate with staff for assistance. Parking and traffic flow are also essential aspects to consider in the construction of a self-storage facility.

A recommended parking ordinance would involve one space per employee during peak hours, as well as additional spaces for customers and temporary use. For multi-story facilities, it is crucial to plan for elevators or lifts during pre-construction to avoid any potential breakdowns.

With the rare a necessary of land, many self-storage facilities are now multi-story, making elevators a necessary component for customer satisfaction.

Ultimately, the key factors to consider for your self-storage facility are convenience, ease, security, and accessibility for your customers. Strive to provide these elements to stay competitive in the market.

Quarterly contracts are often the most economical option. For an additional cost of approximately $50, remote monitoring can also be incorporated. Elevator lobbies play a vital role and should be spacious, easily accessible, well-lit, and sheltered from harsh weather conditions.

Snow guards are an excellent precautionary measure, but certain factors must be taken into consideration, such as your roof warranty, as any alterations or modifications could potentially void it.

It is imperative to carefully select a retention system that comes with its own warranty. Furthermore, it is essential to research your local building codes, as they vary from municipality to municipality. Lastly, it is recommended to purchase from a reputable vendor to ensure the quality and reliability of the product.

CHAPTER 8

MARKETING AND ADVERTISING

Simplify it!

Before beginning construction, make sure to display a "Coming Soon" sign at the site with a contact number and opening date. Include the name and contact number for the new facility, along with an appeal to reserve space now.

This will help attract potential customers in need of storage in your market area. Use this opportunity to secure pre-lease agreements and boost cash flow. Consider hiring a manager before the site is ready to open. This allows for a smooth transition, setting up systems and taking reservations.

The manager can also visit other sites for competitive research and ideas for facility improvements. Obtain your "Certificate of Occupancy" for the facility and manager's apartment before the units are ready. This will help you stay organized and focused on leasing. Start planning for the grand opening and begin advertising. Order business cards, brochures, and other promotional materials. Ensure your website is ready to take reservations. These tasks should be completed a month before opening.

Don't forget the importance of signage, as it accounts for almost half of a facility's business. Reach out to nearby retail outlets to leave brochures in their lobby. The grand opening is a crucial part of the marketing process and sets the tone for the facility.

Even if attendees don't use the facility, they may mention it to others. Planning for the grand opening should be two months before the actual opening to allow for leases to be taken and any issues to be resolved. Take a couple of months to plan for the event, including coordinating a ribbon cutting with the Chamber of Commerce and inviting local dignitaries. This can generate interest and even result in media coverage. Make the event family-friendly and themed to the facility's name.

CHAPTER 9

OPERATIONS, MAINTENANCE, AND UPKEEP

Operations, maintenance, and upkeep are crucial elements of effectively managing your facility.

As such, this section provides valuable guidance on how to run your facility efficiently.

Create a comprehensive binder containing essential information such as contact numbers, site plans, banking details, file locations, multiple hard copies of forms, and operational guidelines.

It is essential to establish a daily checklist, especially if your manager excels at multitasking. The binder serves a dual purpose, acting as a centralized location for all operations and providing a crucial reference tool when hiring a relief manager.

Additionally, it is recommended to create a vendor binder containing information on regular vendors. Keep a well-organized contact list on your computer with customer information and maintain both digital and physical files with care. It is advisable to store most of the information on your computer for easy access and quick printing, with regular backups to avoid any data loss. Regular walk-through checks of unit status should be conducted every 3 to 4 days, with detailed notes taken on any issues that require immediate attention.

During these checks, any problems can be promptly addressed, ensuring smooth operation. It is essential to follow up these walk-throughs with a brief report, detailing the observations made and the actions taken to resolve any issues.

To improve efficiency, consider purchasing postage online from www.usps.com. This allows you to print receipts, order forms, labels, and envelopes, streamlining the process for when customers arrive to move items into their unit.

When customers park their RV or boat for the first time, it is recommended to accompany them to ensure they are comfortable and familiar with the process. For proper maintenance, HVAC checks should be done monthly, with necessary filter replacements and servicing.

Conducting a Sale/Auction: As part of managing your business, there may come a time when you must initiate an auction. This typically occurs when a tenant has failed to adhere to their lease agreement, and you have followed all necessary procedures as per state regulations.

Keep in mind that in some states, having a licensed auctioneer is required in order to call it an auction. Alternatively, if it is referred to as a "lien sale," it is typically handled similarly to a garage sale. Due to the potential for legal disputes in this area of management, it is crucial to adhere to all rules and regulations.

However, it is also necessary as there are professional buyers who actively seek out these auctions. These buyers then resell the items they acquire through platforms such as eBay or flea markets. In order to attract these buyers and possibly even reward them, it is important to plan and promote the auctions in advance. This can be done through maintaining a mailing list and offering incentives such as refreshments or the use of a move-in truck.

Coordinating with other self-storage facilities in the area can also be beneficial, as buyers can visit multiple auctions in one trip. On the day of the auction, it is important to stay organized and provide potential buyers with a set of rules and guidelines.

It is also important to be courteous and friendly, perhaps even offering a flashlight for easier inspection of items and units. These buyers are valuable assets to your business and should be treated as such.

By maintaining a professional and well-organized approach, you can potentially increase attendance at future auctions.

Pest Management:

Implement a highly effective program for controlling pests. This is a crucial matter that requires careful monitoring. Conduct consistent on-site evaluations so that necessary deterrents can be applied as frequently as needed. Even in the absence of any signs of bugs or critters, regular treatments are recommended. Ensure that your clients are familiar with your facility's storage policies and procedures regarding pest control. They should be informed (via their paperwork) to avoid leaving cardboard or paper on the unit floor.

Critter management is another compelling reason to keep your property clean both inside and out. Unoccupied units must be thoroughly swept, including the interior of roll-up doors.

After sweeping and cleaning, apply insecticide and place a small bag of rodent poison inside the unit. Remove cobwebs from corners, light fixtures, ceiling fans, perimeter lights (inside and outside), and any other visible areas. Regular sweeping and mopping in all customer access areas is crucial. Ensure that dumpsters are regularly checked and kept clean with the lid closed. Some facility owners prefer natural methods of dealing with pests, such as Cedar Oil. This not only prevents moths from lingering but also controls other specific insects. It is most effective in enclosed spaces and does not require any permit or license.

However, it should be noted that this approach repels pests rather than killing them. There are other natural products that are effective in eliminating mice and other rodents. One of the benefits of using natural repellents is that they serve as an alternative to chemical insecticides and pose no harm to human health or the environment.

Mold Prevention:

Mold can develop due to various reasons, such as rain or plumbing leaks, condensation, floods, faulty sprinkler systems, and excessive humidity. It is essential to have good insurance coverage for these events. While mold may not be specifically covered, it can be included under "sudden and accidental events," such as flooding or pipe breakage.

The insurance company will determine the extent of coverage and may have a limit. If mold is detected, it is advisable to call a professional team for testing and remediation. If caught early, it can be cleaned with bleach and water before it becomes hazardous.

To prevent mold growth, regularly inspect for leaks and address them promptly. Proper unit ventilation is also crucial.

Managing Operational Expenses:

Unlike other expenses that may vary, insurance costs remain fixed regardless of occupancy. To maximize benefits such as borrowing power and sales proceeds, it is important to minimize operational expenses wherever possible.

This includes carefully monitoring insurance expenses, especially if there is a possibility of selling the business in the future.

Developing a strict budget and sticking to it is crucial in anticipating and managing cash flow challenges that may arise during business cycles. It is recommended to create a cash flow budget at the beginning of the year to accurately forecast potential low cash periods on a monthly basis.

Analyzing Cash Flow:

Self-storage businesses can be lucrative, but they may also face cash flow difficulties. The key to successfully navigating through these obstacles lies in forecasting and managing the various elements that contribute to a business's funds. Utilizing a cash flow budget can provide valuable insight into the next month, six months, or even a year's worth of cash flow. There are several online sites that can assist with forecasting. This approach is particularly useful in preparing for potential challenges, such as the construction of a competing facility, and can aid in determining appropriate rental increases.

Maximizing Cash Flow:

Another strategy to manage cash flow is to delay payments as long as possible. Rather than paying a bill 15 days early, utilize electronic funds transfer to make payments on the due date. This allows for current payments to suppliers while retaining the use of funds for as long as possible.

When selecting suppliers, it is important to consider not only the price but also their payment terms. Additionally, consider leasing instead of purchasing equipment and furniture, as this can help minimize upfront costs and improve cash flow.

Maintenance for Different Parts of Your Property:

Roofs:

Stay on top of your roof maintenance by creating a seasonal plan. Regularly inspect and check the seals every few months. Keep an eye out for any signs of leaks and remove any items that do not belong on the roof. Be sure to also watch for any pooling around objects and tighten screws, as well as check the guttering system.

Don't overlook any necessary repairs, adjustments, or everyday upkeep tasks.

Familiarize yourself with any specific requirements from the manufacturers.

Walls:

As the seasons change, it's important to check the insulation in your climate-controlled buildings.

Test it by hand to ensure the temperature remains consistent across the entire wall. If the insulation is uniform, the wall temperature should be too.

Interior Hallways:

Keep your interior hallways clean by preventing mud and other seasonal debris from being tracked in. Install mats and shoe-cleaning items outside of entrances and be prepared to sweep more frequently if your facility is in a windy area.

Pipes:

Be mindful of potential issues with pipes during freezing temperatures. Have your landscaping company blow out the water from your sprinkler system and turn off the water to any areas that do not need it during the colder months. Insulate any exposed pipes and reset timers in the spring.

HVAC:

Regularly check your HVAC system, as most utility companies offer affordable maintenance services. A properly functioning air conditioning system is crucial in preventing mold and mildew. Be sure to clean the drains and drip pans at the beginning of summer to avoid algae growth.

Gates and Lighting:

Don't overlook the maintenance needs for gates and lighting, as problems may not always be visible. Perform routine maintenance on gates, including cleaning and lubricating tracks, chains, and joints. Be sure to also reset automatic light timers with the changing seasons.

Maintaining Pavement, Landscaping, and Snow Control:

Conduct regular inspections on all concrete and asphalt surfaces. Watch out for fissures and potholes as these can be caused by weather or aging. It is crucial to address any signs of deterioration or cracking as soon as possible.

Preserving the Aesthetic Appeal and Functionality:

Proper upkeep of the landscaping is essential. Clear away fallen leaves, replace wilted plants and shrubs, and treat weeds while nourishing the lawn with fertilizers.

In the summer, adjust the watering schedule to early mornings or evenings to allow the water to seep into the roots before evaporating.

Embracing Technological Advancements and Tools:

Efficiency is key, not just for staying trendy. The self-storage industry has recognized the benefits of technology in saving time, money, and increasing sales and productivity. Many operators have opted for hosted applications, eliminating the need for costly software.

Accounting applications are a popular choice, with some packages offering full hosting suites that come with 24/7 monitoring. Do your research on "hosted applications for self-storage" to learn more.

Leveraging Email for Business:

Emails are not only a convenient way to communicate, but they also serve as a record of communication. With the ability to reach your entire mailing list at once, it's a powerful tool for managing your business.

Keep in mind that emails are legally binding and much faster than traditional mail. You can also use email to send payment reminders, reducing delinquencies.

Adapting to Market Demand:

Flex-Space Technology, also known as Removable Metal Partition Walls, offers a flexible solution for self-storage facilities. This allows operators to adjust unit sizes to meet market demand. It's best to incorporate this technology during the design phase to ensure proper door access and compliance with fire codes.

Enhancing Communication and Security:

Enabled Intercom Systems not only allow for two-way communication and background music but also come with a remote dialer feature. In case the manager is unavailable, the system can call their cell phone or PDA.

Wireless Unit Door Alarms are also a reliable option for security, which can also serve as a marketing tool.

Staying Mobile and Connected:

Investing in a powerful notebook PC allows for mobility and the ability to visit other facilities and conduct field spotting.

With WI-FI networks, customers can access the internet from your PC, making it a valuable asset for your business.

Boost your competitive edge with Plasma Displays. These innovative screens not only showcase your security features, but also make a powerful statement during customer presentations.

Logi-Tech now offers 24/7 monitoring of temperature and humidity levels through a telephone modem connected to the system.

This advanced technology automatically records and troubleshoots readings, ensuring optimal performance. For added security, consider installing a remote-controlled lock system, available through a partnership with a local technology company.

With Track-it, Inc.'s patented multifunctional switch, you can easily activate and deactivate alarms, control lighting, and even turn off the AC when a door is opened.

Self-Service Kiosks with Video Conferencing are the perfect solution for unmanned locations. These kiosks feature two-way video conferencing with a manager at a central location, adding a personal touch to transactions. In today's world, where safety is a top priority, this feature has become an invaluable asset for self-storage facilities as it helps to deter criminal activity and reduce delinquencies.

Thanks to advancements in internet technology, making rental decisions has never been easier or more convenient.

Digitech International offers a system that seamlessly integrates video surveillance and access control. All access log activities are automatically time and date stamped on the video, providing a comprehensive record of activity.

Tailgating has been a major concern for businesses in the past, but with the latest Anti-Tailgating Systems, this threat is greatly reduced. These devices open the gate approximately 13 feet and then, using electronic sensors, detect when a vehicle has passed through and begin to close the gate.

To ensure maximum effectiveness, be sure to post signs on both sides of the gate.

Technology is constantly evolving, and it can be overwhelming for business owners to keep up. Stay informed about the latest advancements and carefully consider how technology can streamline your processes, improve customer service, and attract new clients.

However, it's important to only incorporate technology that makes sense for your specific business needs. Choose wisely and reap the benefits of a more efficient and advanced operation.

Perform Regular Audits:

Conduct audits twice a year on a timely basis to ensure successful operation. These audits maintain specific standards and procedures, clarify any misunderstandings, identify discrepancies, and aid in developing strategies to enhance policies, procedures, and revenue.

Unannounced Audits:

Surprise audits are conducted with minimal notice for the manager, depending on the property size and vacancy. This allows for all vacant units to be inspected.

Three-fold Audit:

The audit comprises three components. The space audit involves a thorough inspection of each unit to ensure accuracy with rental agreements and computer records. The site audit includes assessing curb appeal and maintenance, while the choice audit covers procedures, rental agreements, delinquencies, auctions, and reports.

Sample Space Audit Checklist:

To meet customers' expectations of a clean and organized storage facility, site audits cover all external areas and features that are likely to be noticed.

It is essential to view the property from a customer's perspective.

- Clean curbs

- Well-maintained golf carts

- Visible and legible door and storefront signs
- Welcome/hours sign

- Payment drop box

- Credit card logos

- Functioning neon open sign

- Manager on property sign

- Properly displayed signs and banners

- Working main logo sign lights

- Gate sign with access hours

- Keypad instruction signs

- Welcome sign at the entrance

- Thank you sign at the exit

- Weekly updated reader board

- Non-faded promotional signs/banners

- Clearly marked customer restrooms

- Annual inspection for fire extinguishers

- Clean HVAC filters and proper thermostat settings

- Well-maintained perimeter fence, free of vines and weeds

- Lubricated and properly adjusted gates - Treated for ant infestations

- Clean dumpster area

- Functioning property lighting after dark

- Neat and trimmed landscaping

- No safety hazards in external areas

- Clean and well-stocked public restrooms

- Clean and well-lit corridors, hallways, and stairwells

- Debris-free gutters and roofs

- Removal of any abandoned items on the site
- Prompt removal of any graffiti

- Clean sand urn at the choice entrance

- Clean windows and storefronts

- Working gate codes for the management team.

Audit of Office Procedures This audit encompasses a wide range of procedures, policies, delinquency management, auction processing, and reporting.

It is recommended that every property has a comprehensive workbook that can aid a relief manager and anyone who may need to run the store in case of an emergency.

This workbook contains important information such as the bank's location, post options, golf cart and model bay availability, as well as the layout of the shop and box storage area. It also includes directions to the store from various public roads, a map, and the location of electrical boxes and water cutoffs.

Additionally, there are blank pages for notes to be exchanged between the choice manager and relief managers to ensure effective communication.

Below is a sample checklist for the office audit:

- Review the store information workbook

- Conduct a cash drawer count and reconcile with daily business transactions

- Count petty cash and reconcile with receipts
- Verify timeliness of bank deposits

- Check phone settings for day and night messages

- Ensure Workman's comp notice and business license are prominently displayed

- Check for prepackaged rental agreements

- Review rental agreements for completeness
- Verify all customer information is accurately filled out

- Ensure customer and manager signatures are present

- Check for attached change of address forms
- Verify a minimum of three telephone numbers are provided

- Evaluate the readability of all documents

- Check for expiration dates on any specials offered

- Compare rent amount to computer records
- Confirm lien holder information is completed

- Ensure vehicle VIN and customer photo are on file

- Verify photos and valid IDs of all other customers are on file

- Review and update computer records

- Evaluate the cleanliness and organization of the customer service area

- Verify merchandise inventory records are accurate

- Check that merchandise is properly displayed with pricing

- Confirm the auction schedule is prominently displayed

- Review the current auction advertisement

- Check for any updates to company manuals
- Ensure manuals for operations, auctions, marketing, and comparable surveys are available

- Conduct a computer check

- Verify the absence of games, videos, and CDs

- Review computer notes for all collection calls

- Add late fees and auction fees to delinquent accounts

- Complete Exceptions Activity Report with notes for any variances

- Use the Manage Summary Report to compare previous month's figures

- Review Standard Rents Report to analyze free and below market rents

- Review the Market Summary Report

- Change HVAC filters

- Ensure a polaroid camera and film are on hand.

The Final Step of an Audit: After conducting an audit, the next crucial step is to develop a detailed action plan outlining necessary task, responsible parties, timeline for completion, and a follow-up date one month after the new audit.

It is imperative to distribute this action plan to the store manager, area manager, and any other relevant personnel. Clear assignments must be made to address any identified issues, and a follow-up date should be set to ensure completion.

Audits play a vital role in providing owners and customers with quality service, as they help identify areas for improvement. Managers are not infallible, so it is important to recognize their diligent efforts.

Additionally, the audit process can aid in decision-making regarding underperforming employees. Although audits can be time-consuming, the benefits they bring make them well worth the effort. For assistance with audits, consider utilizing the services of reputable companies such as syrasoft.com, smdsoftware.com, spacecontrol.com, storeman.com, domico.com, and digitech-intl.com.

CHAPTER 10
ADDITIONAL
SECURITY MEASURES

Additional safety protocols must be implemented to ensure the protection of both employees and customers in the event of a rare armed robbery.

This includes installing an alarm system in the establishment and manager's residence, as well as utilizing webcams for audio and video surveillance that can be monitored remotely.

To discourage potential robbers, a visible sign stating that the business does not keep cash on hand should be displayed. In the event of a robbery, employees should remain calm and follow a pre-determined plan discussed in a meeting.

This includes activating the alarm discreetly and calling for assistance through a walkie-talkie or intercom. If a weapon is present, remaining slow and composed is crucial, as the perpetrator may be agitated and unpredictable.

After the robber has left, the police should be contacted immediately, and no evidence should be touched.

Detailed descriptions of the incident and the perpetrator should be recorded by both the manager and employees to aid in the capture of the suspect. Surveillance footage should also be secured and reviewed for further details. The use of digital recording devices is recommended for better playback and duplication of footage for the authorities.

The incidence of this particular type of crime is generally declining, and the self-storage industry is not as affected as other businesses.

However, it is important to remain vigilant for obvious reasons. For instance, it is crucial to consider the public's response and ensure the safety of your facility, as well as your proper actions.

Customers must have confidence in the security of your facility.

Those with advanced security measures such as individual door alarms and numerous cameras seem to have fewer issues. On the other hand, facilities with limited security measures are experiencing an increase in break-ins. In these instances, perpetrators often breach the property's perimeter, often by cutting through the fence, to search for small items they can sell at pawnshops or other outlets.

One common scam to watch out for involves paying tenants who rent a small unit to gain access to the property. They often loiter and observe what other tenants are storing and where. They then return and conduct a large-scale break-in by targeting multiple units and quickly leaving the premises.

Another emerging trend is the use of lock-cutting tools to create tunnels through drywall, allowing the perpetrator to access multiple units down a hallway. This results in losses for both the facility and its tenants.

Another vulnerability to consider is the use of counterfeit money, money orders, and fake receipts by individuals. These customers take a receipt from the facility, scan it, and manipulate the text or create a replica on their own computer. By simply changing the date, they can make it seem like they have paid for months in advance. To prevent this, facilities can use watermarked receipts to verify the authenticity of payments.

Criminals are attracted to self-storage facilities due to the expensive high-tech equipment being installed. They often target cameras without serial numbers, which they can easily steal by climbing onto the roof. The threat of computer viruses is also on the rise, posing a potential danger to any business.

To protect against this, it is crucial to regularly update anti-virus software and have a firewall in place. Additionally, strict policies should be enforced to prevent employees from using company computers for personal activities such as checking personal emails.

Self-storage operators are now taking security measures more seriously, especially in light of potential terrorist activities. Background checks and other initiatives aimed at deterring terrorists from using self-storage as a hiding place for their bomb-making materials and supplies have become essential.

In the past, self-storage facilities were the go-to spot for terrorists due to the lack of security measures. However, with the implementation of these measures, the likelihood of this happening has decreased. Background checks are an essential part of this, as terrorists usually do not have a credit history or references.

Furthermore, they are aware that smaller self-storage facilities in remote areas may not conduct these checks. Hence, it is crucial for managers to be able to determine if a potential customer is legitimate or not. Maintaining strict standards in the screening process can help weed out potential terrorists.

Additionally, managers should also be vigilant and pay attention to their surroundings, as this can deter disreputable customers. Employees should also be trained to identify, and report prohibited materials on the premises, such as gunpowder, PVC or metal piping, and dismantled kitchen timers. Maintenance crews should also be trained to recognize suspicious behavior, such as strange smells or sounds, irregular schedules, and heavy foot traffic on the property.

Self-storage managers should conduct routine checks on locks and can even invite the local police department to use the facility as a training ground. It is essential to have a checklist when closing the facility to ensure its safety. However, it is crucial not to oversell the security measures in place, as this can have legal consequences.

Managers should also not allow the police to intimidate them into opening a tenant's unit without proper documentation, such as a court order or search warrant. In case a lock needs to be cut for any reason, the manager automatically becomes responsible for the contents of that unit and may violate the tenant's rights. It is essential to familiarize oneself with the laws of the state regarding such situations.

CHAPTER 11
EMPLOYEES

When moving forward with your self-storage facility, it is crucial to assemble a competent team. Strategize where to recruit and how to train your staff. An initial decision to make is who will manage the facility on a daily basis. You have the option of hiring a manager, taking on the role yourself, or hiring a management company.

Hiring a management company means they will handle staff recruitment and supervision, which may be a better approach for large facilities unless you have experience in this area. Additionally, a management company can assist with the grand opening and reservations. For a facility with an average size of less than 40,000 square feet, a two-person team will be necessary before obtaining a "Certificate of Occupancy." This team will handle tasks such as sales, leasing, marketing, maintenance, audits, and landscaping.

If the facility is larger, consider hiring a team of three or four. Keep in mind that these facilities typically operate from 9 a.m. to 9 p.m. Monday-Saturday and 1 p.m. to 5 p.m. on Sundays.

If an on-site apartment is included in the facility, hiring a couple is recommended. Otherwise, two unrelated individuals can share the workload by overlapping their schedules for three days and working solo for four days.

Your manager should possess strong marketing skills and attend regular meetings with local business groups, including the Chamber of Commerce.

During the construction phase, the manager can also assist with tasks such as numbering units and hiring landscape personnel and can even take telephone reservations.

When hiring, remember to prioritize attitude over skill. The ideal self-storage manager should have customer service, sales, marketing, computer, and accounting skills.

They should also be able to multitask and effectively manage the facility as if it were their own. Additionally, it is important to have a relief (part-time) manager on standby.

All employees must agree to a background check as part of their application process. It is essential to assess their honesty, integrity, and abilities, and to have a 90-day probationary period in place. Be sure to have your attorney review the application to clarify details such as your right to terminate and the employee's responsibility to vacate the apartment within a specific timeframe.

Other important documents to have in place are the employee handbook, operations manual, and employment agreement. Seek guidance from your state's self-storage association for assistance with these.

Lastly, ensure that your manager is familiar with the state's lien foreclosure process as outlined in the state statute.

Important qualities to look for when hiring include:

- A positive attitude

- Maturity in handling difficult individuals

- Adaptability

- A customer-centric mindset

- Strong communication and sales abilities

- A sense of pride in personal appearance, often indicative of how they will maintain the store

- Self-motivation

- Authenticity

- A managerial mindset, including the willingness to accommodate those who arrive near closing time

- Organizational skills

- The ability to see both the big picture and pay attention to details.

What is appropriate compensation for managers? The salary should reflect their hours, the size of the facility, and whether they reside on-site. It is crucial to calculate the required hours for completing assigned tasks and provide a fair salary and bonus structure. The average salary in the United States is typically between $25,000 to $35,000, with a lease bonus percentage included.

Training managers for a new location:

Make it clear to employees that they are the face of the facility and play a crucial role in creating a positive first impression.

This is essential for customers to feel valued, safe, and treated courteously, resulting in a positive experience with customer service.

Conduct pre-scheduled training sessions or seminars and provide a well-organized handout for reference. Walk through all procedures from the customer's arrival to departure, ensuring they leave with a smile.

Mystery shopping:

This practice involves hiring an independent individual to assess how well managers and other employees are performing their roles. The "mystery shopper" pretends to be interested in renting a storage unit and asks various questions to evaluate customer service and other areas.

This should be included in the employment agreement, disclosing the use of recordings or secret shoppers. As the owner, it is your responsibility to inform potential employees of this practice during the hiring process.

Many industry vendors offer these services and provide detailed reports, recordings, or CDs to the owner and on-site manager.

Hiring and training for success:

The ultimate goal of any self-storage business is to generate profits, and this is heavily reliant on having professional and capable managers. As such, it is the owner's duty and objective to hire top-notch, marketing-oriented managers for newer facilities that are essentially retailers in every aspect.

"Efficiently reduce employer liability by acknowledging that there are no legal restrictions, either common or Federal, against employers monitoring employee email and Internet usage.

As the computer or network belongs to the employer, all information transmitted through it is their property. While email can serve as a social activity among employees, it can also be a waste of time and expose the employer to potential legal issues such as sexual harassment or defamation of character.

Employers are also accountable for any copyright or trademark infringements committed by their employees during daily business operations. It is prudent for employers to monitor employee email in order to mitigate potential liabilities arising from employee actions.

However, it is crucial to inform employees of this surveillance. Another measure to lessen liability is to include a disclaimer (available at emaildisclaimers.com) at the bottom of every email sent through company systems, tailored to address relevant legal aspects of the business.

Here are some safety tips for individuals in the self-storage industry:

- Remain vigilant of your surroundings at all times.

- Make photocopies of customers' driver's licenses before taking them to view units.

- Trust your instincts.

- Avoid entering units while showing them to potential renters.

- Do not show units after dark.

- Provide managers with cell phones for emergencies.

- Supply managers with key fobs that connect to the alarm system.

- If permitted in the area, encourage managers to carry mace on their keychains.

- Install cameras at the main entrance to capture a clear image of individuals entering. - Place keyhole cameras on keypads for a full-face shot.

- Have a camera in the office with a video display screen for the manager's use.

- When inspecting the property, use a golf cart instead of walking.

- Keep hallways straight to eliminate hiding spots for criminals.

- Install phone lines in display units.

- Keep fake "dummy" videos on hand to provide to criminals who request a copy of the videotape.

- Install glass storefront windows at exits to allow passersby to see inside.

- In the event of a robbery, step away from the cash register.

- If being robbed, request to be locked in a unit.

- Attempt to take note of the perpetrator's height and physical characteristics.

- If witnessing a crime, do not confront the perpetrator. Instead, take note of their physical characteristics and license plate number, and call 911."

Consider walking the premises in pairs, if possible. Before accessing a unit, thoroughly inspect for any unusual wiring. (In the past, there have been reports of renters running meth labs from their storage units, rigging doors to explode upon opening.)

Managers should always carry cell phones with them and have at least two forms of communication available. Foster a positive relationship with your local police department.

Prior to patrolling the site, inform management of your intentions. Conduct training sessions and rehearse emergency procedures for potential robberies. When walking, stay in the center of the aisles and avoid being near unit doors.

Develop safety manuals and train employees on how to handle various situations. Encourage managers to enroll in self-defense classes. To minimize the risk of theft, vary the days and times of cash deposits.

After auctions, promptly deposit funds into the bank. Remember, employees are valuable assets. Treat them with respect and reward exceptional work, but also be aware that your business is an asset to them as well."

CHAPTER 12
CUSTOMER RELATIONS

Building strong customer relationships is crucial in today's society where convenience and quality service are highly valued. Failing to meet these expectations can easily lead customers to take their business elsewhere. It is essential to understand the wants and needs of potential customers and strive to fulfill them with a warm and friendly attitude.

Maintaining a clean, welcoming, and safe environment is also vital for customer satisfaction.

Even when faced with challenging customers, it is important to treat them with the same level of courtesy as friendly ones.

Asking questions and actively listening to their concerns can go a long way in meeting their needs.

Remember, unsatisfied customers may not voice their complaints but can still damage your facility's reputation through word-of-mouth. Therefore, it is crucial to train employees to provide excellent customer service and avoid arguments, even with difficult customers.

When possible, bending policies to accommodate a customer's request can help maintain their satisfaction. Instead of passing off customers to other salespeople, it is best to handle their concerns oneself and show genuine interest by repeating and clarifying their needs.

Building strong customer relations also involves regularly reaching out to customers, expressing gratitude for their business, and addressing any questions or needs they may have. Sending thank you cards can also foster long-term positive relationships. Every customer should be greeted with warmth and respect, making them feel like a valued friend. Simple gestures like standing up, smiling, shaking hands, and introducing oneself can leave a lasting impact on customers and contribute to a positive experience.

While managing customer conflicts, it's important to demonstrate your capabilities in solving their storage issues while also making them feel valued and comfortable. Focus on the problem at hand and avoid taking things personally but be assertive in setting boundaries. Use clear and direct language, without resorting to analogies or figures of speech. Instead, ask them directly what they want and need from you in order to find a mutually beneficial solution.

Remember, customer complaints are an opportunity for improvement, so always listen to feedback. After addressing their concerns, show them the unit they will be leasing and document the conversation for future reference.

When they reach out to you, be prompt in returning their call. By handling conflicts professionally and keeping emotions in check, you can reach a resolution that benefits both parties.

Always approach the situation with a business mindset and avoid getting personally involved. Effective communication and understanding the root of the conflict will help you find the right solution.

Remember, it's crucial to have a strategy in place for resolving customer disputes and remaining calm and respectful during discussions. Choose a quiet and private setting, maintain open body language, and actively listen to the customer without interrupting.

If you find yourself feeling angry, try to handle the situation calmly by using positive body language, smiling, and slowing down the conversation.

Avoid placing blame on others and take responsibility as a member of the facility's staff. Less than 10 percent of customers actually express their dissatisfaction with management, which means that most customers will simply choose to go elsewhere.

Conducting a customer survey is an effective way to gather feedback and ensure that your facility is meeting their needs. Consider using the analogy of a restaurant in your survey and invite both current and former customers to participate voluntarily.

Clearly communicate your goal of constantly improving their experience and keep the survey concise and focused. Another important aspect of customer service is to be flexible, such as waiving late fees for a customer's first late payment.

This demonstrates understanding and customers will appreciate it. However, if late payments become a recurring issue, you can explain that the computer system only allows for waiving late fees once every few months and you are unable to change this.

CHAPTER 13
INSURANCE CONCEPTS

Understanding Insurance: Are You Fully Protected? The cost of premiums and insurance coverage can vary depending on your state.

Factors such as construction type, location, square footage, and liability limits all play a role in determining the level of risk. As a new self-storage operator, it is crucial to seek professional advice early in the construction process to assess potential risks.

Your agent can assist in determining the appropriate coverage and limits and may also offer recommendations to help prevent costly claims.

It is important to note that your claim history will impact on your future premium costs. Therefore, it is essential to have the right insurance coverage in place from the beginning.

Here are the basic types of insurance you will need: Property Exposure: This type of insurance covers the physical property on your premises and should be based on replacement cost. The replacement cost is not the same as your home's replacement cost, so it is important to stay updated on rising construction costs and adjust your policy accordingly.

Coverage for:

- Fire
- Smoke damage
- Wind damage
- Hail damage
- Theft
- Vandalism

Business Interruption:

This insurance protects against the disruption of your business cash flow. For example, if a hurricane damages your facility and causes a collapse of buildings, you may experience a temporary interruption in revenue.

Business interruption insurance is designed to provide continuous and uninterrupted revenue, for a predetermined period of time, typically one to one and a half years. General Liability:

This type of insurance covers lawsuits and provides protection regardless of fault. It can be beneficial in situations such as slip and falls or damages caused by access gates. Crime: Sale and Disposal:

This insurance protects against negligence when disposing of tenant's property. The regulations for this vary by state, so it is important to follow proper procedures to avoid legal action.

In the event of a lawsuit, this insurance can cover legal costs, up to a predetermined limit for one year. In conclusion, it is crucial to have the right insurance coverage for your self-storage business to protect against potential risks and costly claims.

Seek professional advice and regularly review and adjust your policy to ensure you are properly covered.

Liability Coverage for Customer Goods:

This policy provides protection in case of loss or damage to a tenant's property. It safeguards against any negligence on the part of the operator that may result in such a loss.

In the event of a claim, it will cover the cost of repairing or replacing the tenant's property.

Other Coverages Included:

In addition to customer goods, this policy also covers automobiles, workers' compensation, employer practices liability, and claims of wrongful termination (typically for larger facilities).

It also includes protection for incidents of sexual harassment and systems breakdown, including HVAC and electronic security systems and gates.

Umbrella Policies:

This type of policy combines various coverages into a single package. It can include computer systems and other considerations, and provides extended liability limits for general liability, auto liability, and a portion of worker's compensation.

Keep in mind that increasing the deductible may lower premiums, but you should ensure that you can afford to pay the deductible in case of a claim.

Limited Pollution Removal:

In the event that a customer leaves behind a pollutant, this policy covers the cost of cleaning up and removing it.

Many commercial insurance companies require proof of ability to pay the deductible before providing coverage. It is important to get multiple quotes with different deductibles to find the best fit. Specific Limits and Occurrence Basis:

When determining the coverage and limit amounts needed, consult with your agent.

Most policies have a specific dollar limit and are written on a per-occurrence basis with an aggregate limit. Make sure the aggregate limit is higher than the occurrence limit to ensure maximum protection.

Tenant Insurance Paid with Rent:

Rent tenant insurance is an additional income source for facility operators and serves as a risk management tool rather than a profit source.

Coverage is offered at the point of lease and is written on a group insurance policy.

Customers pay an extra amount along with their rent, and the facility may earn fees for offering this protection.

This type of insurance is permitted for non-licensed facilities, but regulations are becoming stricter.

Some states offer a simplified insurance license for self-storage facilities to help reduce liability for tenants' property.

Seek Professional Advice:

Given the complexity and constantly changing landscape of risk management, it is important for self-storage business owners to seek the advice of a qualified insurance professional who is familiar with the unique exposures of this industry.

CHAPTER 14
LEGALLY THINKING

"Juridically Pondering The Liability Law has undergone revisions that favor the plaintiff, necessitating a thorough understanding of these amendments as it signifies the property owner's negligence.

Previously, the courts placed the burden of proof on the plaintiff, who only had to establish that the owner/management neglected to address an issue before a person suffered an injury, such as a fall. Now, it is imperative for management to identify and rectify potential liabilities and problems.

The plaintiff only needs to provide evidence that the condition existed for a considerable amount of time.

Inquiries like, "How frequently does the management instruct employees to inspect the premises and address potential hazards?" have proven successful in some cases, arguing that owners have a duty to conduct regular inspections in areas accessible to the public.

Courts distinguish between two types of notices:

Actual and constructive, where the former occurs when a customer or individual informs the management of a potential issue, and the latter is when a defect persists for an extended period.

If the facility has sound policies for inspections and maintenance, these problems are promptly addressed, and warning barricades are put in place until the issue is resolved.

Security gates must also be regularly maintained to prevent personal injuries. The most common incidents involve bodily and automobile damage, as a malfunctioning gate can close too quickly and cause harm.

It is crucial to have signs on both sides of the gate indicating that it is only for vehicles and not for pedestrians. Maintenance and repair records should also be kept."

Risk of Liability For Property Damage and Loss:

This is another potential liability concern. If a tenant's belongings are disposed of due to a breach of the lease agreement, the tenant may file a claim against the facility for lost goods. This issue should be addressed during the leasing process, and tenants should be provided with a list of safety and security measures.

Other Legal Recommendations:

It is advisable to have separate ownership for the facility and the land, rather than having them under the same corporate structure. This can protect you in the event of a major lawsuit.

Additionally, it is a good idea to install fake cameras on the property to give the impression of extensive security and surveillance.

However, it is important to inform tenants about these cameras in the lease agreement. If the cameras are not monitored regularly, this should also be disclosed to customers.

Environmental Liability:

Mold damage has become a major concern, similar to asbestos. Exposure to mold can cause damage to both property and people. Mold thrives in environments with a relative humidity of 60% or higher, so it is important to address this issue promptly.

Leases and rental agreements should have specific exclusions from liability for mold damage, and customers should be made aware of the risks of storing items in a property susceptible to mold growth.

It is crucial to control the relative humidity in climate-controlled units and promptly fix any water leaks in the building's roof, eaves, and foundations. Installing humidifiers can be effective if they are suited to the building's needs and properly installed.

Damage Caused by Customers:

When damage occurs due to a tenant's actions, the key question is who is at fault and liable. Depending on the extent of the damage and the circumstances, the facility owner can either file an insurance claim or cover the cost of repairs themselves. It is important to establish who caused the damage and hold them accountable.

The lease agreement should clearly outline the expectations in such situations.

To handle damage issues, there are two options available:

Either add the repair cost to the tenant's rent if it is a minor amount or restrict their access to the property until it is resolved. A well-drafted lease with appropriate terms can effectively resolve such matters. As soon as any damage is discovered, it is crucial to promptly inform your insurance agent, regardless of the deductible or extent of damage.

This is usually a requirement by insurance companies. When leasing the unit, remember to inform the tenant that storing hazardous materials, such as flammables, in the facility or other tenants' spaces is strictly prohibited.

Limiting the value of items that tenants can store is essential. The lease should specify a maximum value, typically $2,500 (unless an addendum agreement is made), for items stored in the facility. While you do not assume liability, this sets a limit.

Additionally, provide the tenant with an insurance brochure and offer them the option to secure coverage for their belongings at a small premium, up to the agreed amount.

The lease should also include language that prohibits storing items with sentimental or unknown resale value.

It is advisable to suggest to the tenant that they acquire their own insurance for items valued higher than the allowed amount in the lease clause.

This helps to limit your exposure and sets a cap on the amount the customer can sue for in case of liability. The insurance company determines the actual cash value (ACV) based on the replacement cost less depreciation. The clause should clearly state that the tenant cannot sue for an amount exceeding X, even if you are found liable.

The aim is to create several barriers between you and the tenant to minimize potential legal issues. While no lease can guarantee complete protection, these inclusions can make it more challenging for tenants to cause legal problems.

Legal Trends in Self-Storage:

In light of past incidents, it is crucial for self-storage operators to prioritize customer screening, hazardous materials monitoring, and liability release provisions.

Many companies, such as the Self-Storage Association in your state, offer background checks for added security. It is important to observe the behavior of potential renters and obtain a "red flag" list from local or state police agencies.

Additionally, it is advisable to include a clause in the rental agreement that releases the operator from any liability, which is legally binding in most states if clearly stated in the contract.

Assisting the authorities with legal matters is a responsibility we should all take seriously. As the owner of the property, you have the right to provide the rent roll to the authorities as the tenant is renting a unit from you. This helps the authorities with their subpoena or search warrant requests.

However, it is important not to succumb to pressure and show a tenant's property or unit without proper paperwork. Officers should present identification and the appropriate paperwork, and it is advisable to note down their name, badge number, and the purpose of their visit to protect yourself in case of any court inquiries.

A subpoena is a legal command that requires someone to appear or for the authorities to access their personal property at a designated time and location for a legal matter. Unlike search warrants, subpoenas do not require immediate action, giving managers time to consult with the owner, management company, and their attorney.

Search warrants, on the other hand, are issued by a judge and require immediate action, allowing the police to search for a specific individual or property for evidence of a crime.

Before any potential search takes place at your facility, it is essential to have a well-prepared plan and a thorough checklist. As a manager, it is your responsibility to carefully review all pertinent documents before proceeding.

It is important to maintain a helpful, calm, and courteous demeanor throughout the process. If the search warrant permits the police to seize business materials, such as rental agreements or customer information, remember to provide them with copies rather than originals. In the event that surveillance footage needs to be copied, have the necessary equipment, such as a computer or

VCR, ready to transfer the footage onto a CD or videotape.

If this is not possible, the police may take the original recordings, compromising your files. Once the search is complete, make detailed notes of the events and the items that were provided to the authorities.

If possible, make copies of the search warrant and record the names and badge numbers of the officers involved. In case any objects are taken from the premises, ask the police to create an inventory of those items. It is crucial to be thorough and meticulous when documenting the incident. In situations where lock cutting may be necessary, it is still uncertain whether it is permissible.

However, if a methane laboratory is involved, it can pose a significant danger. Therefore, it is imperative to be as cooperative and helpful as possible, as the police are present to protect the public.

Should self-storage facilities accept packages given the intense competition in the industry and the increasing number of pharmaceutical companies renting storage units?

This practice may pose risks and classify the facility as a bailment business, as self-storage is primarily defined as renting real estate for storage purposes.

Although pharmaceutical tenants are desirable, accepting packages would entail entering their units and assuming responsibility for the contents, which goes beyond the duties of a self-storage operator. This could expose the facility to liabilities such as damages, theft, and damages to the packages.

Additionally, accepting cash payments and holding keys to units can also increase liabilities. One solution could be investing in an automated locker system, although it may be costly.

Another option is to require cash payments to be made in person with a receipt issued, or using a self-storage kiosk which records payment details and provides receipts. Late fees can also be regulated by the state, and to avoid any potential issues, the leasing agreement could include a clause allowing the facility to charge the tenant for late payments made using credit cards.

Lien Auctions:

In nearly 46 states, the self-storage operator holds the authority to conduct a lien auction of a tenant's belongings in case of lease default. It is vital to consult with your legal advisor on the appropriate course of action.

Adequate notice must be given to the tenant that a lien auction will occur within a specific number of days after the default. It is essential to outline the specific state statutes in the tenant's lease agreement. Please refrain from referring to the lien sale as an "auction" unless a licensed auctioneer is involved.

Bankruptcy Filing by Tenant:

It is crucial for self-storage operators to be well-informed on how to handle a tenant's bankruptcy filing.

Firstly, the type of bankruptcy must be determined as different provisions apply to self-storage operators under the automatic stay. Seek legal guidance and obtain relief from the automatic stay through court proceedings to regain possession of the rental space. This will ensure the smooth running of the facility.

CHAPTER 15
RENTAL/LEASING AGREEMENTS

Agreements for renting or leasing storage units can be obtained from your state's self-storage association, which is an invaluable resource for new storage facility owners.

To ensure compliance with federal and state laws, it may be necessary for your facility to conduct a pre-rental screening.

Before finalizing the agreement, it is important to have your attorney, who has experience in the self-storage industry, review and approve it.

This document should be well-crafted to protect the interests of both the owner and the tenant.

The self-storage lease should cover various important aspects such as the length of the agreement and its renewal clause, specifying whether it is on a month-to-month basis or longer and the due date for payments.

It is crucial to include a clear termination date and avoid using the term "anniversary" as it may limit the ability to increase rent.

The lease should also provide for the right to terminate with a notice period and a renewal date.

The agreement should clearly define the purpose of the storage unit, which is intended only for storing personal or business property and not as a warehouse.

It should also list items that are prohibited from being stored, such as hazardous, flammable, or noxious items, as well as irreplaceable items with unknown value or emotional significance.

This serves to prevent the use or creation of items within the storage unit. Including the exact language from the Comprehensive Environmental Compensation & Liability Act (CERCLA) for the definition of "hazardous materials" is important and may be required by the mortgage and insurance carriers.

The lease should also specify a dollar value limit for stored items and require express written permission from the facility to exceed this limit. The lease should state the owner's right to control access to the facility, either through electronic gates or sign-in procedures during specific hours.

However, this may be subject to change in case of an emergency. The lease should also mention any exceptions to gate hours in case of emergencies or power failures, and the owner's right to deny access to the tenant in case of default.

Ensure that the lease contains appropriate release language to absolve the facility from any liability for personal injuries and fatalities of individuals at the premises, as well as for property damage or loss caused by various factors such as fire, water, acts of nature, theft, burglary, vandalism, malicious acts, mysterious disappearances, or rodent damage.

It is crucial to include these releases in separate paragraphs to comply with state regulations. Some states may require a clear and prominent statement at the beginning of the lease, informing the customer of the facility's right to enforce a lien. Additionally, the lease must specify the facility operator's right to enter a storage unit in case of emergencies, government requirements, and other limited circumstances for inspections or repairs.

It should also include a clause outlining all the situations that would be considered a default under the lease, not just non-payment of rent, but also failure to comply with other lease obligations.

It is advisable to include a provision for subletting and to consult with an attorney to establish a mediation or arbitration clause. This adds an extra layer of protection for the facility, as the tenant would have to go through the mediation or arbitration process before taking legal action.

The lease must also state that all information provided in the lease and any other documents related to the rental are accurate and truthful. The rental agreement is the primary means of protection for the facility owner and should be drafted carefully by a lawyer with experience in self-storage law.

It should clearly define the facility's role as a landlord, the tenant's risk of loss, and the necessity of insurance for the stored property. Furthermore, the lease should outline the rights and obligations of both parties and the consequences of non-payment of rent.

It is crucial to include a statement clarifying that the facility owner does not assume care, custody, or control of the tenant's belongings. The lease should also include a provision limiting the facility's liability for the stored property. It should specify that the value of the items stored cannot exceed a certain amount unless approved in writing by the facility owner.

Customers may store items with a higher value if they provide proof of insurance for 100% of the estimated value and agree not to store items with sentimental or emotional value unless they waive the right to make emotional attachment claims. Last but not least, the lease should include a jury trial waiver provision, depending on the state's laws. This clause limits the tenant's right to a jury trial in the case of a claim and should be reviewed with legal counsel.

Include a specific section in the lease that clearly outlines the tenant's release of liability towards the landlord. This means that the tenant is solely responsible for any risks associated with storing their belongings, and the landlord cannot be held accountable for any loss or damage caused by burglary, disappearance, fire, water damage, rodents, or acts of nature.

Additionally, the lease should state that the landlord will not be held liable for any loss or damage to the stored property resulting from the active or passive acts, omissions, or negligence of the landlord, their agents, or employees.

Furthermore, it is crucial to include a clause regarding tenant insurance. It is the tenant's responsibility to obtain insurance to protect the value of their stored property, and they assume full risk for any loss or damage to their belongings.

The lease should also include a provision that waives subrogation, meaning the tenant's insurance company cannot pursue claims against the self-storage facility after paying out any claims. For kiosk or internet leases, it is necessary to add a statement stating that by pressing the "accept" button, the customer is indicating that they have carefully reviewed and found the terms and conditions of the lease agreement to be acceptable. They also agree to abide by and be bound by these terms.

This statement should also make it clear that the customer's ongoing payment of rent constitutes their continuous acceptance of the lease terms, including any future modifications of which they will be notified at least 30 days in advance.

CHAPTER 16
RENTAL RATES
AND INCREASES

"Setting Appropriate Rental Rates: Avoid the mistake of undervaluing your product. Many business owners mistakenly equate excellent customer service with sacrificing profits.

Do not mistake being competitive for pricing your product too low. Focus on providing exceptional customer service while also ensuring a profitable bottom line. Determining rental rates should only be done after conducting thorough research on the market and assessing the added value of your facility.

Conduct a comparative analysis of other facilities in your area to gauge both the demand and competitiveness of your offerings. This should align with your cost evaluation and profit goals.

Keep in mind that rental rates are influenced by the law of supply and demand and can fluctuate based on market conditions and the economic climate of the local community. Remember, lost rent cannot be recovered, so it is crucial to stay updated on your competition.

Rental rates should be based on market demand, not just occupancy. If your facility is at full capacity, you are not maximizing your income potential and may be inadvertently creating competition.

Stay adaptable to setting rates and stay informed about market changes. Long-term rental trends should be adjusted upwards to remain competitive and profitable. It is wise to maintain rates between the highest and lowest prices in your area, taking into consideration the amenities and location of your facility.

Pricing should serve as a starting point, with the ability to adjust as needed. Keep in mind that you can raise the rent on existing customers with just thirty days' notice. Choose a pricing strategy that suits your business and your market. With a common-sense approach, you can find success."

Maximize your income potential by improving your investment through added amenities. If your facility has consistently high occupancy rates and you have not raised your rent, you may be undervaluing your property.

It is common for prices to increase over time, and staying in line with market demand by implementing rate hikes can help maintain the value of your facility. This is especially important if you plan on selling your business, as not increasing rental rates could lead to lower offers from potential buyers. Ultimately, tenants will either adapt to the new rates or choose to leave. However, even a small increase in rent is preferable to the hassle and cost of moving. Plus, if they do choose to move out, there will likely be others willing to pay a higher rate for your facility.

Don't miss out on potential revenue, especially when it comes to attracting buyers. Even if you plan on passing the facility down to your children, it is important to maintain or increase its value.

Keep an eye on your competition to stay informed about market changes and be prepared to market the unique advantages of your facility. Ask yourself important questions such as whether you are the newest facility in the area, if your location is better than your competitors, and if your management excels in areas such as marketing.

While it may be tempting to offer the lowest prices in the area, don't undervalue your facility. Your competitors are likely waiting for you to raise your rent so they can do the same, as this is a common practice in the business world.

Develop a strategy for managing rent hikes. Will residents receive an annual increase or smaller, semi-annual increments? Determine the percentage and timing of the increase, considering its impact on your financial bottom line.

Review the length of stay for your tenants and assess how long they have been paying the same rate without any changes.

Consider sticking to the most popular unit mixes and increasing rates more frequently. This way, if some tenants do move out, you will have new residents moving in at a higher rate. The increase can be implemented all at once or seasonally during the busiest time of year. To minimize the impact on customers, consider small, incremental increases instead of one large one.

Calculate the difference between their current and new rates to determine the most appropriate approach. Train your staff on how to handle the increase, emphasizing the importance and benefits of such changes. They should use tact and confidence when communicating with residents.

Provide incentives for your employees to handle this change effectively. They can also provide you with a list of tenants due for an increase.

Demonstrate the value of the increase to customers by investing in visible facility repairs and upgrades. This can help them understand and accept the increase more easily. If possible, start these improvements before notifying tenants of the increase.

Evaluate the results after each rate increase, tracking complaints, move-outs, and occupancy levels. This will allow you to adjust your strategy accordingly. While there is no one-size-fits-all solution to keep everyone happy, consistency is key.

CHAPTER 17
EXPANDING/REMODELING
OR ADDING ON

Adding Value:

Another strategy to stay ahead or outshine your competitors is to revamp or expand your establishment. You can also elevate the value of your self-storage facility by offering additional services. While certain upgrades may not directly increase your property's worth, others can.

Don't miss out on the opportunity to earn more by implementing improvements or broadening your services. Take a closer look and strategize on what will boost your profits.

With careful and strategic planning, you can boost occupancy rates and generate higher rental income. Rather than simply keeping up with the competition, aim to provide the best possible facility. Assess your curb appeal and approach your facility with the perspective of a potential customer.

Evaluate your first impression. Keep in mind that drive-by traffic comprises a significant portion of the self-storage business. Don't overlook the second impression, which encompasses your staff, customer service, and the cleanliness and brightness of your reception area.

Pay attention to the condition of your units and buildings. Keep in mind that women's opinions can greatly influence others, especially when it comes to the appearance and cleanliness of your facility. If you plan on expanding, start considering it once your occupancy reaches 60 percent.

Some Tips to Increase the Value of Your Facility:

Controlled Environment: (Refer to chapter 3 for a comprehensive guide on controlled environment) Have you observed if your competitors offer controlled environment and if so, how occupied are they?

This contrast can assist you in determining how to promote your units with controlled climate. If you don't currently have any, consider constructing a few and then analyze the results to determine the optimal number to meet the demand.

Tenants who require storage for electronics, furniture, art, and other valuable possessions belong to a higher income bracket. Businesses often require this for their furniture, fixtures, pharmaceuticals, cosmetics, and other retail items.

These tenants typically have longer tenancy and are more reliable. They specifically seek out units with controlled climate. The size of the unit mix is relatively similar, ranging from ninety square feet to one hundred and thirty square feet. Larger units are more prevalent in rural areas. Controlled environment facilities usually have a higher demand for larger units. If you're planning to construct a new facility, it's essential to note that the basic building costs should have an additional 15 percent for controlled environment features.

Marketing your controlled environment units can significantly benefit your business. Utilize flyers, mailers, and emails to reach out to potential clients in your area and educate them about the advantages of these units. It's crucial to do this regularly.

You can also visit or call professionals in the business district, informing them that you have ample units available due to the growing demand for controlled environment units. When promoting these units, avoid using only the term "Controlled Environment."

It's important to highlight the significance of humidity in these units and refer to them as "Temperature and Humidity Controlled Units." This will effectively convey the unique selling point of your facility.

Incorporating Retail into Self-Storage: Are you familiar with Retail or have you considered it as a means to enhance the profitability of your self-storage business?

The answer hinges upon your individual business style and capabilities. While this amalgamation is gaining popularity, there are both advantages and disadvantages to consider.

You could opt for a strip mall in front of your self-storage facility, with the entrance leading to the storage units, while also offering customers the convenience of shopping and dining at your café. This also serves as a form of advertisement, as satisfied customers will spread the word.

Regardless of the approach, proficient management is crucial. This skillset will cater to the needs of both the retail and self-storage aspects. In the event of renting out any or all of the retail spaces, you can manage it from a central location.

You have the option to include a variety of businesses such as a postal center, café, donut shop, nail salon, or even living quarters on the upper level. The initial impression and aesthetic appeal of your facility is a valuable asset.

Each business will benefit from the exposure of the others, creating a cohesive image. A significant financial benefit of this mixed-use retail facility is the use of triple-net leases to offset expenses.

Consult your CPA regarding this, as it typically includes common area maintenance and property taxes. Vertical Expansion: As land prices continue to rise, many developers are turning to multi-story buildings. These structures are more cost-effective when it comes to heating and cooling. If there is available space on your property, this is a viable option for expansion. Record Storage: With the evolution of digital storage, record keeping has also evolved.

However, businesses still require secure off-site storage for physical copies. Film Preservation: Preserving film requires specialized knowledge, as it must be kept in cold and dry airtight vaults.

Word-of-mouth and referrals are the best forms of marketing for this niche area of expertise, and timely delivery is essential. Medical Records: Handling medical records necessitates specialized training to adhere to security measures outlined in the Health Insurance Portability and Accountability Act (HIPAA).

Wine Storage:

The demand for wine in the United States has been steadily increasing over the past decade, with consumers now storing approximately 10 percent of their purchases.

As a result, the number of self-storage facilities offering wine storage is on the rise. This trend is expected to continue as the U.S. market expands. While this may seem like a lucrative option for facility operators, it is important to note that wine storage caters to a niche market and may not be suitable for everyone.

There are three main aspects to consider when it comes to wine storage:

Controlling the climate.

Ensuring security.

Complying with alcohol laws in the state where the facility is located.

For valuable insights into this specialized niche, your local wine merchant is a great source of information and can also serve as a valuable referral source.

Additionally, customers who store wine are less likely to default on their leases. However, if a client requests direct shipments to the facility, it is crucial to be aware of federal regulations and seek proper legal counsel.

One common mistake made by new entrants in the self-storage industry is assuming that they can easily add wine storage to their unit mix and achieve success. This is not always the case.

Wine storage is a highly specialized offering and requires a specific target market to be successful. It is best suited for affluent areas, such as resort destinations where people bring their own wine, or upscale neighborhoods where wine enthusiasts may not have the space for their own wine cellars.

In coastal regions with yacht marinas, wine storage can also be a draw for those with onboard wine cellars.

Proper wine storage involves keeping it in a clean, dark, and humid environment with good ventilation.

The ideal temperature for wine storage is between 50 to 55 degrees Fahrenheit, with minimal fluctuations. Therefore, it is crucial to provide a vibration-free environment.

For example, a slight change in temperature from summer to winter, around 10 degrees, may not significantly affect the quality of wine.

However, a sudden increase of 10 degrees on a daily or weekly basis can be problematic. Maintaining proper humidity levels is also crucial for wine storage. While the acceptable range is between 50% to 80%, the ideal humidity is 70%.

Due to the delicate nature of wine, facilities that offer wine storage have contingency plans in place to regulate temperature and humidity in case of a power outage.

These storage areas are typically isolated from the rest of the facility and have their own entrance with specialized security measures. To ensure maximum security, some state-of-the-art facilities have also implemented biometric scanning in high-security areas. In recent years, there has been a growing trend of incorporating mobile storage options, where containers are delivered and picked up from businesses and homes.

While the self-storage industry is still debating the feasibility of this approach, it is becoming increasingly popular. Many view it as a valuable business opportunity that sets their facility apart from competitors. However, this option requires more land and increases overhead costs.

Proper management skills are also essential for successfully operating a mobile storage operation.

Self-storage facilities are increasingly offering truck rental services, which has become a common expectation among customers. This added convenience can bring in potential leads and boost occupancy rates by up to 25%. Furthermore, it presents an opportunity to sell packing supplies like boxes and tape, generating an additional $1,500 per month per truck. Utilizing the truck's exterior space for advertising can also promote your business.

Consider partnering with a truck leasing company, such as U-Haul, which offers an advertising program for dealer trucks with a minimal cash investment.

However, it is important to thoroughly research this venture, as it comes with its own set of challenges and requires efficient management and salesmanship. On the other hand, car washes can provide an immediate and steady cash flow, making them a valuable investment.

This all-cash business requires minimal labor and continues to generate income even when the facility is closed. Additionally, it is recession-proof and offers tax benefits through equipment depreciation.

Moreover, if the self-storage facility is ever sold, the car wash can add value to the property. Careful planning is crucial for the car wash's layout, considering factors like future expansion and turning radius. Approval from local authorities is also necessary for drainage and access.

The cost of constructing and equipping a self-serve car wash bay can range from $25,000 to $30,000 per bay, while automatic car washes are significantly more expensive. However, banks typically offer financing options with a 20-30% down payment.

Alternative: The surge in cell phone usage has created a pressing demand for additional telecommunication towers. These structures, typically standing between 100 and 200 feet tall, have recently been made shorter due to advancements in technology.

One profitable option for self-storage facilities is to lease space on their properties for these towers, as they are often located in zones that are favorable for such structures.

Unlike traditional towers, disguised options such as pine trees or flag poles can be approved in a shorter timeframe.

Furthermore, while each cell phone company may own their own tower, many companies that specialize in building and leasing towers will rent out multiple slots to different cell phone providers.

This presents an opportunity for self-storage owners, as each company leasing a slot will also need to rent storage space for their equipment.

Negotiations can also include annual increases in lease payments, and contracts can specify that each company renting a slot must also rent a minimum amount of storage space. In the event that a tower is no longer in use, the contract can require the company to pay for the restoration of the storage unit or forfeit it to the self-storage facility for potential future use.

However, it is important for self-storage owners to be aware of FCC regulations, which state that a carrier must be present on a tower, or it must be taken down. This can give cell phone companies a sense of power in negotiations, though the only minor drawback to this arrangement is the need for after-hours access for wireless companies.

Advertising boards:

There could be limitations and neighborhood constraints regarding the placement of advertising boards.

These factors significantly influence the location of the board. Familiarize yourself with the available choices as you may receive a proposal for development. Safekeeping boxes: Although constructing them can be costly, safekeeping boxes can generate substantial profits.

It is essential to have a secure safe with a sturdy vault door. To determine the demand for safekeeping boxes, you can check the waiting lists at nearby banks. Inquire about the necessity by discussing your plans.

Conduct thorough research on companies that offer fireproof boxes and determine the popular sizes in your area.

Storing firearms: You have three options:

- Have the client complete and sign a standard lease.

- Politely decline, saying "No, thank you."

- Or find a middle ground and include special provisions for this specialized storage.

There is no right or wrong answer; it ultimately depends on the owner's preference and risk tolerance. Storing firearms is not illegal if they are legally owned. Whether for hunting purposes or part of a valuable collection, self-storage facilities provide a secure location for gun owners to store their firearms, and in turn, offer self-storage operators an additional niche market to explore.

Some individuals appreciate the fact that they can store their firearms away from their home and out of reach of children. This also protects their guns from potential loss in case of a home burglary.

If your state or region is known for hunting, firearm storage could be a valuable marketing opportunity. Consider reaching out to gun clubs and insurance agents to promote this service. A major selling point is the potential insurance discount homeowners can receive by storing their valuable guns in a high-security facility outside of their home. It is crucial to not allow illegal firearms in your facility.

For example, storing sawed-off shotguns, firearms with unpermitted silencers, and short-barrel firearms, along with weapons such as brass knuckles and switchblade knives, is strictly prohibited. However, storing a hunter's dove shotgun for the season is acceptable. It is vital to be able to identify an illegal firearm, and your clients should be escorted by trained employees when storing their firearms.

In light of the prevalent concern over terrorism, it is prudent to discourage individuals from hoarding a large number of firearms. This can be achieved through the inclusion of a special clause in the lease agreement, known as the non-bailment by operator clause. This provision makes it abundantly clear that the landlord does not have any responsibility or control over the tenant's firearms.

The tenant, in turn, assumes all risks associated with the loss or damage of their firearms, including but not limited to fire, water damage, natural disasters, or theft. It is also crucial to have a separate insurance provision in special leases, especially considering the potential value of collectible firearms and other valuable items.

Additionally, it is necessary to include a requirement for the separation of ammunition from firearms and ensure that all firearms are appropriately registered. In the event of a lien sale, the laws regarding the sale of firearms vary from state to state.

However, most local jurisdictions have procedures in place to verify the registration of a firearm to a specific tenant, allowing the manager to remove the firearm from the unit until the time of the lien sale.

If the tenant pays the outstanding balance and reclaims their possession, the firearm can be returned to them. In some states, such as Texas, selling firearms at a lien sale is not considered illegal, as long as it is done occasionally and without a license. Furthermore, if a safe is already being used for storage, it can also accommodate wine storage in the same area.

Executive Suites:

Many owners of self-storage facilities are now offering choice and suite leasing options. These suites come with added benefits such as a shared kitchenette, restrooms, a conference room, and a staffed reception area for receiving calls and welcoming clients.

Some facilities even offer additional amenities like high-speed internet access, secretarial services, and mail services. Postal Services:

Postal services have become increasingly popular among self-storage owners, creating a new opportunity for growth in this industry. Some owners have gone the extra mile by establishing an official U.S. Postal Choice branch within their facility, which adds value and increases traffic (usually over 500 per day).

However, it is important to ensure that the facility has adequate parking and meets government standards, especially if the government needs another facility in the area. Start-up assistance is available from companies like Plano in Texas, but it is important to have the resources and manpower to handle the additional workload. Training for new employees can be obtained from the local post choice office, and at least 750 square feet of space is required to qualify. The entire process can take up to six months, and the facility must also comply with Americans with Disabilities

Act regulations for parking and access. Adding a postal facility to your self-storage business can bring in an extra $3,000 per month, including retail elements commonly found in post choice branches.

The government also pays a percentage of the postage sales, making this a profitable venture for facility owners. Consider these opportunities for expanding, remodeling, or adding significant value to your self-storage facilities.

Are you considering the self-storage industry as a potential opportunity for yourself? Over the past few years, we at American Steel Buildings, Inc. have received countless inquiries, which have inspired us to create this book. Our aim is to provide a starting point for your exploration of this industry, as there are numerous profitable possibilities waiting to be discovered.

You could start small in a smaller town and use it as a source of income for your retirement or as a successful business venture. Alternatively, you could dive right in, do your research, and build a large and lucrative enterprise. Whatever you decide, we hope this information will assist you in making an informed decision.

Key Questions:

Some of the commonly asked questions we receive include:

What exactly is the self-storage industry?

Where did it originate from?

What is its future outlook?

What are the advantages and disadvantages?

Should I take a more serious look into it?

Where should I begin?

How should I get started?

While this book may not address all your specific needs, it is an organized overview to stimulate your thought process. You will come across the phrase "do your homework" throughout this book, as it is crucial to conduct thorough research before making any decisions.

This could involve attending self-storage seminars, trade shows, and utilizing online resources.

The self-storage industry is a major consideration for any business venture. It is now up to you to determine what it can offer in terms of fulfilling your dreams. Please note that I cannot be held responsible for any profits or losses incurred in this field.

This book is not intended to serve as a warranty and any resemblance to other published information is purely coincidental.

My research and experience have led me to interact with numerous like-minded professionals and authorities.

It is advisable to consult with experts in each area of your inquiry, as this book is simply a guide and not the ultimate authority.

Ultimately, you are the best judge of your own situation.

Final Thoughts:

You now have some tools at your disposal, so go ahead and explore the self-storage industry. I wish you all the best in your endeavors. If you need any further assistance, please do not hesitate to reach out to us.

Contact Details:

American Steel Buildings, Inc.

www.gosteelgo.com

sales@gosteelgo.com

800-400-5121